IS THE U.S. BROKE?

THE SURPRISING

ONE PAGE FIX!

(AND WHO CAN FIX IT, BUT MORE IMPORTANTLY, HOW WE, THE USA VOTERS, CAN MAKE IT HAPPEN!)

By

Fred Graham-Yooll

11:30:18

Independently published

ISBN 9781790578146

Printed in the United States of America

CONTENTS

CASABIANCA

The boy stood on the burning deck,
 Whence all but he had fled;
 The flame that lit the battle's wreck,
 Shone round him o'er the dead.

 Yet beautiful and bright he stood,
 As born to rule the storm;
 A creature of heroic blood,
 A proud, though childlike form.

 The flames rolled on - he would not go,
 Without his father's word;
 That father, faint in death below,
 His voice no longer heard.

 He called aloud – 'say, father, say
 If yet my task is done?'
 He knew not that the chieftain lay
 Unconscious of his son.

 'Speak, father!' once again he cried,
 'If I may yet be gone!'
- And but the booming shots replied,
  And fast the flames rolled on.

 Upon his brow he felt their breath
 And in his waiving hair;
 And look'd from that lone post of death,
 In still yet brave despair.

 And shouted but once more aloud,
 'My father! must I stay?'
 While o'er him fast, through sail and shroud,
 The wreathing fires made way.

They wrapped the ship in splendour wild,
 They caught the flag on high,
 And streamed the gallant child,
 Like banners in the sky.

There came a burst of thunder sound –
 The boy – oh! where was he?
Ask of the winds that far around
 With fragments strewed the sea!

With mast, and helm, and pennon fair,
 That well had borne their part,
But the noblest thing that perished there
 Was that young faithful heart.

Felicia D Hemans. 1834

AUTHOR'S ALERT

What should one do if they discover something about trade of great value to our country? Worse, that it might mean the end of America as we know it if the message can't get out to the right people?

Brainwave, why not write a book, but not just any book. Write one with a summary at the front so that any reader can learn the whole story of trade and wealth from it, with the rest of the book explaining the details and the evidence.

Mission accomplished, everyone is immediately alerted and knows what we need to do in seconds. After that, it is up to the reader to decide whether they want to learn more. The point being the Alert has been sounded with the proof at hand.

§§§§§

SUMMARY

My own introduction to this subject came when I was researching the life of Queen Cleopatra of Egypt (51-30 BC). A simpler time, it allowed me to learn the secrets of her success, and more on that later. Learning the making of money by a nation was just as important as the gaining of wealth by individuals, those riches led to power and the gaining of respect from those around them such that it frequently resulted in leadership and with it, world dominance by that country. Curious, I followed the trail of that story of our World to modern times, and apart from war, the status of a nation's balance of trade was the best predictor of who was going to be the world's next leader.

Now we come to modern times and the story of the USA today. Most Americans have no idea of what has happened or why. Indeed, we are being constantly reminded by our leaders that we should be helping others less fortunate. These same people are living in a 'Dreamworld'. Perhaps wealthy themselves, or perhaps in privileged positions, or even worse, living that life on borrowed money, that message has been repeated so often that it has become almost an accepted fact.

Reality is like a cold shower in the morning. It wakes one up suddenly with little or no warning of what lies ahead. Unhappily it is an apt description of where we are in the USA today, with the UK our bedfellow, and Canada and Australia not far behind.

$$$$$

So what have I learned, for I am no Politician or Economist and only a hard working guy, now retired, and watching his savings disappearing over time. What I found was simple but took a long time to uncover. There is only one thing that can bring a country to its knees, BRIBERY AND CORRUPTION. After that there are three main things that can bankrupt a country:

1. Overspending one's Budget to the point one has used up all one's money with nobody willing to lend you more.
2. Having a currency that is flawed.
3. Having a continuous negative balance of trade.

The USA today has a Gross National Product (GNP) of $17.3 trillion which for Europeans means GNI. Next, forget the Debt Clock, for we are only interested in Book numbers. Current Government Debt is $14 Trillion, of which all of it can be easily balanced by the Country's physical assets. Now let's stand back and try and understand why our Government's accounting system was set up the way it is. Can you imagine a relatively simple time with no mechanical calculators: never mind computers, for complicating the books with things like assets, liabilities and depreciation would have been almost impossible. In modern times that is no longer an excuse. I submit that our Government's accounting system should be changed to include the listing of assets and liabilities with depreciation and write offs to come up with a modern balance sheet. There is absolutely no excuse in not having a set of books that can show whether or not a Government is able to borrow money and at the same time show investors the risks associated with those loans. To say a Nation such as the USA cannot afford to borrow when its GNP is $17.3 trillion and its debt $14 trillion is absurd. Not only that, if the money was for infrastructure improvement, that would be akin to having a mortgage on one's house, a fairly safe investment covered by solid assets. Adding another twenty trillion dollars of debt for that purpose, especially if the investor was mostly oneself, should provide our Government with enough funds to move our country from the fossil fuel burning era into one of renewable energy. There is now only one flaw in that argument; the cash drain taking place in trade.

$$$$$

On the second subject thankfully I have nothing but good to say for our currency and its management. To put into perspective its fiat based system and to do away with those proposing we go back to gold or other precious metals, let me relate why Rome collapsed. Its currency was based on silver and so its GDP (GDI in Europe) was limited to the amount of silver on hand–a ridiculous idea that said one needs to mine more or steal it (go to war) from some other country. Well they did but ran out of countries to rob!   The other function of our Federal Reserve in more recent years has been to try and stabilize our economy by preventing booms and busts by raising and lowering interest rates. Despite all kinds of fancy maneuvering with the interbank interest rates, the problem has recently come to the surface with a bang. Basically the Federal Reserve has been artificially keeping interest rates low to prevent a spiral of repeating recessions. Knowing they could not go on doing that forever, any time they saw signs of an economic recovery coming they immediately started letting interest rates begin to rise towards their rightful market levels. Thus past moves to correct trade imbalances promising a stronger domestic economy are offset by these past questionable practices. As to the why of GM's latest moves, more on that later for it was not so much what is going on here as what is going on in the exporting countries to here. (S. Korea, Japan, Germany and China, all with outrageous actions and abuses to the idea of free trade!)

On the third item I ran into my first surprise. The lack of data! A jolt, for the USA is renowned for its data keeping. Trade data keeps track of the cash moving into and out of our Country and is divided into two categories; goods (products) and services (Insurance, transportation, etc.). Available monthly and annually and broken down in almost any way one could wish, it never-the-less was like looking at a Bank Statement, but with one key difference; there was no opening or closing balance and was therefore useless in trying to determine where our Nation stood versus the rest of the world! In retrospect, I should have known that it was a deliberate decision that could be laid at the feet of our leaders and politicians, but worse, our economists.

The horror story took years to assemble. The last year that the USA had a positive balance of Trade was in 1975. Starting slowly, but climbing inexorably, that deficit grew as the years went by. I need to stop here and explain something for it is the key to understanding what that meant.

When a country has a negative trading balance, it means that a negative cash flow is occurring. The money is leaving the country and is ending up in the hands of the seller or country that is exporting its products or services, in our case, mainly to China, Germany, Japan, and S. Korea, but also to many others. It is currency that is being removed from circulation in the USA and is no longer here to sustain our economy. It is gone and has reduced our wealth by that much. If large enough, that removal can bring on an economic collapse which our economists call deflation. So how do our economists respond? One can start up the printing presses, but we all know that leads to our currency declining in value and this time our economists call that inflation: a no win situation. Well we know that has been going on, but at the same time not disastrously so, and only gradually. There is only one other way that loss of currency can be replaced: by borrowing from someone, for with trade a seller demands prompt payment unless facing an unusual and rare situation. (See later details.)

I left the most important part of this section to last, for it is the key to understanding why our debt is no longer in the control of the USA. When dealing with trade deficits, most of it is being done by our business and private sectors and except for our military, not by our Government. Those businesses pay for these imports from the profits they make from selling them to we the people of the USA. However, with that number now well over seven hundred billion dollars per year, our treasury is being forced to replace that currency by borrowing lest the USA moves into a deflationary depression due to that currency leaving our Country. Theoretically it can be ascribed to overspending on our Budget, but let's not fool ourselves, that has been handled in a different way and more on that later, for our politicians don't want to talk about that.

Going back to our story, and in the belief by our leaders that our own manufacturing industries were of little importance, our industries now suffered a two-pronged attack from our Government. Here at home (the EPA with its mission of clean-up or shut-down) and this time overseas (via The World Bank and our own Government's financing of new plants in the so called deserving countries of the World), the end result of which was a shutting down of USA manufacturing capacity and its moving to overseas countries where new plants were being built. What followed was a compounding of this blind behavior. Other industries that relied on these basic industries for their supplies, started to follow their exodus. As for the so-called High-Tech industries that were supposed to be the savior of future jobs for the USA's now unemployed, that too became a joke as exporting countries ignored our patents with impunity with none of our leaders or politicians willing to fight to protect them from that theft. That battle over time became more difficult as the importers became increasingly reliant on those sources, and with their donations to our politicians, won their support to ignore the pleas of the now unemployed, which because they had lost their jobs had little or no money to donate to those same politicians re-election needs. Indeed this soon became even more lopsided as those same importers were becoming increasingly wealthy off those same cheap imports.

The above insane story is only matched by what has happened since then, and in some ways what we deserve. That trade deficit, has finally reached the incredible number of between seven and eight hundred billion dollars per year, and if we have the courage, for it takes that, to add it up from 1976 to 2017, it has reached the insane number of twenty-trillion dollars. (That's $20,000,000,000,000 in case you don't know how many zeroes it takes to make it.) Oh, and by-the-by, that includes the five trillion plus of illegal drugs that have been flowing into our Country by Government estimates. By no coincidence our national debt has also reached that insane number, and more about that later, for Budget deficits are financed by our Treasury and Government 'leger-de-main'. Whereas trade deficits are financed by business and private enterprise borrowings. (Again more on that later.)

Compounding the above, even more incredibly no one in our Government seems to realize that while the USA has been pumping trillions of dollars into the Chinese economy over the past twelve years, we are the only ones doing so, for the rest of the World has had a positive trade balance with China! To say our leaders of all parties are (expletive deleted) is an understatement. In other words, in case somebody in our Government has not understood what has happened, we have created this mess all by ourselves with bribery and corruption rampant among those that are making our policy decisions. Sure one could argue that China has not been playing fair by stopping imports whenever it chooses, and if that were not enough, steeling our technology whenever they choose. The point though is that these same lawmakers have allowed it to happen and are still doing so! The fix for this behavior is to make the raising of money for re-election illegal and to cast a vote for any product or subject from which one has received money or a benefit also illegal. Good luck on that one!

Again, I need to explain something else. Most people think our debt is a result of our Government's failure to manage its accounts, giving away or spending that much without having the taxes to cover it. Even the expression 'kicking the can down the road' emphasizes that inability. So, how was it covered? You will not like the answer. By the printing of money (GNP of six trillion dollars in 1976 times a Federal Reserve Bank/Treasury inflation target-varies– of 2% per year equals eight trillion dollars by 2017). The rest came from stealing the money from our Nations Trust Funds and using them to meet budget shortfalls (Social Security, Military and Civil Service Pension Trust Funds, and more on that later). In other words, budget shortfalls were financed by printing money and theft from the Trusts. With our current Trade deficit running at $ 0.7 trillion dollars per year, this is also the rate at which our country will also have to borrow, a rate that is unsustainable without major changes.

Our economists, and most are brilliant, have been playing every type of game to try and neutralize or defer the inept financial behavior of our politicians. From quantitative easement, non-marketable Bonds not in the concept of Federal debt, and artificially keeping interest rates low, these games have only compounded the situation even if delaying the 'day of reckoning', for when they are reversed or corrected, the pressures will be such that the house may come tumbling down. As for the poor lenders holding our debt, the market will lower the value of their debt to a number that can be repaid, with that statement being based on no games being played at that time, something that will almost certainly not happen.

$$$$$

We must now look at the other side of this story, something that is also not pretty. The big three exporters, as I like to call them, are a nefarious bunch with the biggest attributing its success to the evil genius of Nazi Germany under Adolph Hitler and more on that story later. The others are China and Japan. None of these three know or are familiar with the concept of 'Free Trade', for each control the entry of imports into their countries by various means that together replaces the need for tariffs to protect their industries, workers, and accumulating wealth.

Meanwhile in America, with unemployment rampant and distorted to make things look better (If we give up looking for a job, we are no longer listed as being out of a job). Meanwhile, the downward pressure on wages is increasing. The other problem is the illegal immigrant numbers were becoming significant and distorting both wage and unemployment statistics for a job when filled by these newcomers was not captured in many Government statistics. Worse yet, they are not paying taxes for to do so would flag their presence here. Despite all this, they are being enrolled in our schools and in welfare programs and so both Government and State Budgets are becoming increasingly difficult to balance. At this point our leaders and politicians made some fateful decisions. The first was to pressure the Federal Reserve and Treasury to lower interest rates by any means so that interest costs could be artificially lowered and thus Budgets be easier to balance. This was a devastating blow to retirees and others that relied on interest income on which to live, but while known was ignored. The second decision was equally brutal, the decision to change the cost of living index to reduce Social Security payments. The retirees of America soon started to go back to work and in the process worsened the plight of the unemployed. Despite the tax burden falling increasingly on wage earners and middle America, tax breaks were increasingly being given to business and the wealthy on the theory that 'trickle down' economics would be in play, a theory that has since been debunked and in fact only widened the gap between the wealthy and the poor. The reality was in fact quite different. 'Middle America', despite moving from a one income to a two-income family, found the earnings gap instead of closing, widening. (See research using IRS data on the trillion dollars per year shift of income to the 1% elite of America.) Currently, with options running out, in desperation families are moving to on-line shopping in an attempt to lower their costs. That move has meant an even faster shift to imports for these same on-line stores get nearly all their supplies from imports and we have to ask, is this the 'death spiral' in our story.

$$\$\$\$\$\$$

And now to a positive subject and an opportunity to develop 'home grown' industries. Innovation and new technology, two subjects in which the USA has excelled in the past and we see no reason why it cannot do so in the future with only two provisos. They be defined as high National Security Industries with supply mandated from USA owned and operated producers, and that this time patents be observed or imports from violators be banned. The coming innovations are going to be driven by converging technologies that together will result in what I would describe as being our 'Twenty-First-Century Industrial Revolution.' The first discovery has been the fact that the burning of fossil fuels has been poisoning our atmosphere and must be phased out as soon as possible. In the transportation field, the only practical alternative technology available is electricity with all future vehicles powered by that source.

The second converging technology is computer chip memory capacity and the more sophisticated software it can support. With that innovation comes the ability to automate more complex tasks such as the driving of vehicles, planes trains and ships, not to mention more industrial and manufacturing uses. With automated driving will come more shared driving with 'on demand' use making the need to own cars redundant. Only a short step away will be the formation of chains of cars and trucks to speed up travel and to increase energy efficiency. (A 50% energy efficiency improvement while increasing speed from slipstreaming by 33%). At that time will also come dedicated highway speed lanes for that form of transportation diverting 75% of air travel to highway (see later Chapter on the impact on cities of these changes). And so now to the 'One Page Fix'.

$$$$$

1). Legislation be enacted to prohibit all politicians from voting for, or proposing and writing laws to do with any business or company that has given them money for any purpose for the past twenty years. This legislation should include enacting legislation to limit the power of the 'super rich' by limiting political donations to a maximum of one thousand dollars from any source during any election period.

2). Modernize our Federal and State Budgets to include Balance Sheets, Assets, Liabilities, and Depreciation. This way we can allow the upgrading of our infrastructural facilities and the investments needed to move from the fossil fuel age to the renewable energy world we need.

3). On USA State and Federally financed investments of any kind, henceforth all equipment, materials, and manpower will be supplied from USA owned and domestically produced facilities. (Virtually all countries follow this practice.)

4). All military and products deemed to fall into the category of 'National Security' to be supplied from USA owned and domestically produced facilities, with all associated technology to be restricted in its dissemination.

5). All investments associated with the move from fossil fuel use to renewable energy, transportation and production, should be made by USA owned and produced plants including machinery, parts, vehicles, aircraft and ocean vessels.

6). Introduce import restrictions on any country in violation of the principles of 'Free Trade' such as Government protection of their industries by limiting imports by any means including approval by Unions, Guilds, or Committees. Also to include the theft of technology, patents, or copywrite.

7). Implement currency controls to ensure a positive balance of trade is achieved[1] in the event Congress fails to pass trade legislation.

8). The imposition of import quotas on any products that exceed 50% of USA consumption.

9). The imposition of import controls on any food source that exceeds 75% of USA consumption.

10). The President of the USA be granted the power to implement any of the above steps with the exception of items seven through nine which shall be limited to a six month period and then be subject to the approval from the USA Congress thereafter.

$$$$$

BEFORE VOTING, WE AS VOTERS HAVE TO ASK OUR CANDIDATES FOR ELECTION ONLY TWO QUESTIONS: ARE YOU COMMITTED TO SOLVING OUR ENVIRONMENTAL AND TRADE PROBLEMS, AND IF SO, WILL YOU WORK WITH ALL PARTIES TO MAKE IT HAPPEN?

$$$$$

---

[1] See 'Presidential Authority over Trade: Imposing Tariffs and Duties by Caitlain Devereaux Lewis, Legislative Attorney, Congressional Research Service, Dec. 9, 2016.

CHAPTER I

BACKGROUND

When asked by my friends what I was currently writing, surprise that it was about Trade was quickly followed by puzzlement and soon disinterest. Not surprisingly, the business men and women were the ones showing curiosity, but even then, it was almost a 'yawn' subject and of little import. The reaction of the younger was also surprising for theirs was almost like discussing a warm and fuzzy thing, not exactly charity, but almost a social 'doing a good thing.' They thought of it as 'Free Trade' and helping the poorer people of the World to come into the modern age. After learning about the reality of what was going on in our world, that expression was like a knife in my heart, for there is no such thing except perhaps in a dream. Regardless, not one of the many people I have talked to about Trade had the slightest notion of the domino effect it was having on our economy, not to mention the repercussions to our industries on jobs, cash flow, debt, wealth, and leadership. As a writer, I knew I was going to have a battle on my hands to get people's interest in such a mundane subject, not to mention appreciating its vital importance. The words 'Free Trade' were also causing a social disconnect with that idyllic expression making it even harder to refocus attention on what is going on in the real world. Almost ready to give up, the thing that kept me going was the realization that unless we woke up to this danger and soon, we could be facing an economic collapse that would make the 'Great Depression' of the 30's look like nothing.

So, how could we get the public's attention? Well first, the book title and cover were going to have to be something special. After that, the story would have to be simple and clear with the answers providing a constructive way to fix the problem. (For the younger audience and myself).

$$$$$

With that as my starting point, the realization hit me like a brick. Deep down I was trying to discover why a Country, that at one time had been called 'The Greatest Country on Earth' and had rescued Europe and the World from two wars, was collapsing. In fact, what I had discovered was the mechanism that was causing that collapse, but not the reason behind it, and for that answer, I had to thank my love of Roman History. In fact, it was only now, in the sunset of my life, that I was even asking myself why that was so? Dummy, it was because of the great writers and thinkers of that time and the many scholars that have written about it since, all making it one of the most interesting and educational periods. My favorite was Julius Caesar, whose greatest enemy, Cicero, had described him as being one of the greatest writers of jurisprudence Rome had ever seen, with some of those Laws on anti-corruption surviving intact through the ages until Rome's collapse seven-hundred-and-fifty years later. In point of fact, Rome's last remaining Province was Gaul, which became the future home of the Catholic Church. Little appreciated is the fact that Gaul voted to adopt the Roman Constitution[2], including Caesar's Laws of jurisprudence, in its entirety when forming their future nation of France. Thus, the document that Thomas Jefferson studied in Paris was not the same one he presented to the committee here in the USA. I can only conclude he must have been a pragmatic man for he left out of that document not only Julius Caesar's Laws of anti-corruption, but the guidelines of who, and under what conditions, candidates could run for election. They were:

-All candidates would have had to have served a minimum of five years in Rome's Legions or some other public service deemed acceptable.

-All candidates would have had to have served in some lesser position before running for Consul of Rome (The position of Chief Magistrate.)

-All candidates could only run for one term with the running for re-election or the raising of funds for that effort banned.

-All office holders were free from prosecution while in office.

-All office holders performance, while in office, was subject to review by Rome's Senate after their term was completed with censure and prosecution for wrongdoing the consequence.

One can only dream about what the inclusion of those Laws in our Constitution would have meant. No re-election campaigns. The no raising of funds for re-election (Currently taking one-third of the time of all Congressmen and Senators).

Their voting for what is right instead of what pleases voters and the people supplying them with money for re-election, etcetera. What does all this mean? The truism is this: When things go wrong, look first for bad Laws and Agreements,

---

[2] Though in fact not a Constitution as such, but a group of Laws.

for there you will find the flaws. If still unsuccessful, next look for those that are either breaking or circumventing those Laws or Agreements. Only then will you have found the culprit or culprits[3].

The definition of Economics is the study of trade. The definition of Free Trade is the exchanging or sale of goods and services without hindrance, barriers, or taxation. That said, what has been happening?

$$$$$

The 'Big Three' regarding 'Positive Trade Balance' (Surplus of Exports over Imports or a flow of cash into their country) are China, Germany, and Japan.

The 'Big Three', or should it be 'Little Three' of the 'Negative Trade Balance' (Shortfall of Exports over Imports or a flow of cash out of their country) are the USA, the UK, with a tie between Canada and Australia for third.

And here, I would like to repeat a quote from Great Britain's wartime leader, Sir Winston Churchill. And actually, a paraphrase of a quote by George Santayana. "Those who fail to learn from history are doomed to repeat it." How he would be turning in his grave, for one would almost have to be blind not to spot some characteristics in the country groupings.

The 'Big Three' Countries were all at one time under Dictatorships or Centralized Government rule, and by no stretch of the imagination could they have ever been called democracies. In contrast, the second list contains Countries that represent some of the world's greatest proponents of democratic forms of Government. The United Kingdom with its 'Magna Carta,' the USA with its 'Constitution,' and Canada and Australia with their heritage.

That does not mean to say that the former is still dictatorial, but only that some of their past practices have yet to be entirely shed. Nor, and more importantly, does it imply dishonesty, but rather the fact that a period of transition has been occurring with the losers having only themselves to blame for only bad Laws and Agreements the cause.

$$$$$

---

[3] Lest anyone goes away thinking Thomas Jefferson made a mess of thigs, his genius was in separating our Constitution into a separate document that would be hard to change and distinct from Congressional Law making.

The conclusions from the above are that if the World was one Country, we would not be having this discussion, for it would have been between individuals and the fact some were getting richer at the expense of the poorer with no one to blame but themselves. Thus, the flaw in the current system is not the fact there are countries (they only reflect the history of tribes and groups, both local and imposed), but rather that the walls that different currencies have erected have become the ultimate barriers to further trade.   In the case of the USA, with their dollar currency one of the World's back-up ones in support of all the others, if that currency were to fail, then all the others would suffer that same fate up to the theoretical percentage of that support. Unfortunately, that is not how markets react to bad news for they usually over-adjust until they find the right balancing number. In the interim, that over-adjustment could trigger other currency failures which in all likelihood would result in a domino type of collapse with only the strongest ones that were backed up by hard assets and defensive walls surviving.

Allow me now to let you into a little secret. I have gone down this journey many times in my head and know there are simple answers to simple questions with the outcome leading to a far better World than we have now. The challenge will be to get our politicians together and to steer them in the right direction, but perhaps you the reader can help. With that said, "Lay on Macduff."

$$$$$

CHAPTER II

HISTORY OF TRADE

Life would not exist without water. For early humanity though, it was a barrier to travel. However, it soon became a savior.

The battle lines were drawn almost as soon as human beings came out of the last ice age. Food was the issue, to hunt, or to grow it? That was the question but also the problem, for it demanded two opposite and conflicting lifestyles. Each had their set of challenges and problems, with some only becoming apparent many years later.

Hunters came first, living from whatever they could eat, hunt or kill from the land around them. As their numbers grew, and food became scarcer, so expansion into other land areas took place. And here, water became the barrier. Just when the first person thought to grow edible plants from seed is unknown, but archaeologists have narrowed it down to the Middle East. By 7000 BC, those early seeds had reached by land, into what is now central Turkey and the Persian Gulf areas. And here we come to an incredible story. By 6000 BC, those same seeds had reached virtually every island in the Mediterranean Sea. Lost in this stunning revelation is that they had also reached the Thebes area of Egypt, and to the North, Greece, Macedonia, and Austria. The implications are that travel by sea was driven by something else. If so, what was it? No records or evidence of ships have been found for this timeframe. It was the conflict between farmers and hunter-gatherers, and the desperate escape of farmers to safer areas.

Early farmers knew logs would float, and simple rafts or even rudimentary vessels would have sufficed. After all, the choice for these people was to escape or face death. What did they take with them? Food, and of course, their seeds and goats, the very things that in the long run would feed them.

It was not ocean travel for trade, but desperate journeys of escape and survival. Only later, as population pressures outgrew what their island could support, did water travel become one of escape from starvation. Again, though, with perhaps improved vessels, but still only a rudimentary form of a ship.

With early civilization concentrated around the Mediterranean and its rivers, and with trees the only source of fuel for cooking, heating, and materials for home building, these areas were soon running out of wood even in 3000 BC. With deforestation a way of life, soils became increasingly fragile and subject to erosion from both wind and rain. The culprit for what happened next was the goat. They appear to all have 'buck teeth.' In other words, their front teeth are forward in their jaws, giving them the ability to graze grass more closely than other animals. It explains why early farmers liked goats, for they could live off the land when all other animals had given up. But it came at a price. After normal grazing, grass will eventually grow back regenerating the land, and ready to support animal life. However, in the case of land grazed by goats, if you look closely at a picture of one, you will notice how they would have been able to graze grass down to, and including their crowns from which future sprouts grow. Thus, without crowns, the grass dies leaving the land bare, with only weeds or brush left. With the soil now unprotected, rain and the wind soon washed and blew away that soil into valleys, streams, and finally into lakes or seas. Left behind were gravel, rocks, and a few valleys where topsoil had also accumulated. By 2500 BC, most Mediterranean islands were devastated. As for the surrounding countries, they too were in dire straits, with the hilly and mountainous regions disaster areas. Conversely, the Nile Valley was becoming more fertile from the flooding with silt-laden water from the Ethiopian Highlands each year.

In all probability, over this period, the first ships were developed that could transport food to those areas that were no longer able to support themselves. Archaeologists have provided us with the trail of what happened. First came the Minoans (from Mycenae?), who, with fish, home made goods, and artwork, traded them for grain from Egypt and other areas. Then came the Phoenicians, a tribe that originated in central Turkey and carried ocean trade, navigation, ship design, and exploration to new heights. Adopting a practice of extreme secrecy, they were able to set up a trading empire that relied on providing other countries with their services. Setting up harbors and fortified cities in the host countries, (from Carthage, opposite Sicily, to Bahrain in the Persian Gulf, they were thus able to establish a trading empire without having to conquer and dominate the Mediterranean as such. As it turned out, that was their Achilles heel. For with lands being conquered they gradually lost those trading relationships.

The Greeks followed next. With wealth pouring in from Trade, taxes were increased almost on a yearly basis on that sector of their economy. Ever the opportunists, those traders were soon moving their business away from Greece and into a series of fortified Trading Cities. I counted at least nine from Massilia (Marseilles) in Gaul (France), to Naukratis in Egypt. Not surprisingly, Greece, without the taxes on traders, soon became almost bankrupt, and unable to support either an Army or Navy, shortly were conquered by Rome. One has to have a sense of humor, for, in our modern world, Greece has again forgotten its history, for it has taxed its maritime industry so heavily that it too has again left Greece and found a home in Cyprus!

How far did these early traders go? The Egyptian Pharaoh Necho II (610-595 BC.) ordered some Phoenician traders (from Bahrain) to explore on his behalf the Southern Seas. Setting off with three ships, they sailed around Africa, re-entering the Mediterranean through the Pillars of Hercules, (Strait of Gibraltar) and thence on up the Nile to the Pharaoh. This first journey took three years, which soon after was cut to one. The Phoenicians reportedly began trading with the East African Ports of Mosyilium, Opone, Maleo, Sarapion, Mundas, and perhaps today's Zanzibar. Products traded were reported to be cinnamon from China, pepper from India, and even the odd bolt of silk, again from China.

With the destruction of Carthage, by the Romans in 146 BC, nearly all their accumulated knowledge was lost. Turning to a new generation of Greek traders, who had settled in the meantime in Alexandria, there was one called Eudoxus of Cyzicus. (Greeks only had one given name, and to distinguish themselves from others, would often adopt the name of where they originated. In his case, not far from what is today, Istanbul). It was to him that the Pharaoh Ptolemy VIII, in 118 BC turned for help. Written records indicate that Eudoxus sailed to India. He was reported to have been most successful, bringing back a cargo of spices and valuable gemstones, such that the Pharaoh promptly confiscated them. Within the year the Pharaoh was dead, and his wife and young son took over as joint rulers. Surprise, surprise, the next year, his wife, now Queen Cleopatra III, sent another Greek navigator by the name of Hippalus to India, presumably to repeat the earlier success of Eudoxus.

History fails to tell us anything, for his discovery was what made the news. Depending on the monsoon season, the current of the Indian Ocean reversed itself! For six months, it flowed East and then, for the rest of the year, West. By timing the journey, ships could now make two trips per year, a much more profitable business. Interestingly, a few years later, when her son came of age and became the Pharaoh, he promptly murdered his mother. History records the son took no further interest in that trading opportunity.

Fast forward to Ptolemy XII's reign in 80 BC; we come to the next discovery. The Indian Ocean current was part of a huge circular one. In other words, the whole thing reversed every six months. Thus, if correctly timed, ships could again double the number of trips they could make a year to four. Overnight, the economics had changed from overland by camel to ships and sea!

Not too bright a man, Cleopatra's father, Ptolemy XII, now ordered Callimachus, his chief Epistragos (Governor), to secure landing rights to the Island of Socotra at the mouth of the Red Sea. Duly done by 78 BC, with the thought that this would become the future home for an as yet to be built fleet of Egyptian trading vessels. Unfortunately, the island lacked a natural harbor, and without protection doomed this plan. The choice then fell to use Yemen with its major port of Aden, or the land of Kush (Ethiopia/Eritrea) with its multiple choices of ports. By default, this second choice became the area on which the Epistragos settled, for when the Pharaoh's daughter, Princess Cleopatra, fled there later; traders had already made Axsum in today's Ethiopia, their headquarters. In July of 62 BC, Ptolemy XII elevated his Epistragos to the additional position of being 'Commander of the Erythraian and Indian Seas.' Thus, Callimachus became one of the key members of Cleopatra's future administration. More importantly, she was now fully alerted to this incredible trading opportunity at the tender age of thirteen, five years before becoming Queen. Thus, while not starting this trading venture, on being named co-regent three years later, there is no question she supervised its growth into the juggernaut it became. Also overlooked was the importance of owning and controlling the sea transportation system. Almost too obvious for comment is the issue of vulnerability, not to mention security and safety. Well maintained, and efficient shipping is an integral and vital part of Trade and should be part and parcel of any trading policy, especially as it affects pollution control. With our Oceans coming under increasing stress, we should own and operate our fleets with only modern, clean, and safe ships being allowed to transport our goods. If that were not sufficiently convincing enough, all we have to do is look at the story of sea power and how it has influenced civilizations through the centuries.

The miracle of the Nile was how nature flooded the Nile Valley each summer. First washing away all salts and debris, and then, as the flooding slowed and stopped, left fresh nutrient filled silt behind. From then on, all that was required were seeds, water, and harvesting, for people to be able to grow enough on which to live. Everywhere else in the known world lacked the magic of the washing away of debris and salt and the leaving behind of the fresh nutrient rich silt.

When civilization came to Egypt, it was the perfect marriage of the 'hunter-gatherers' and the 'farmer dwellers.' One to provide protection, and the other to provide food, the perfect bartering or exchange arrangement allowing both to settle permanently in the Nile Valley and a self-regenerating agricultural environment.

While many researchers have examined the minute details of how Egypt was governed, its development was an example of simplicity in and of itself. As it grew, inevitably there had to be one protector (the Pharaoh) that emerged as the leader with all the others in support. Coupled with the challenge of the Nile's length and the time it took to travel that distance, Egypt was soon divided into districts (Nomes) over which managers (Nomarchs/Epistragos) ruled on behalf of the Pharaoh. At its inception, anything mysterious or unexplained was attributed to a 'God.' With names being given to each, depending on their sphere of influence. A system of Temples, Priests, and servants arose such that by the time of Egypt's last Dynasty, their power was second only to that of the Pharaoh, with their Temple Guards alone numbering over one-hundred-thousand armed men. Lastly, there were the Pharaoh's delegated leaders of such jobs as head of their Army, Treasury, Agriculture, and Trade. These were called Wisers (Viziers). All of the above were run based on only a few premises:

-The Pharaoh, who was deemed to be a God, owned everything.

-In turn, the land was allocated to each manager such that they would be able to support their activities from barter.

-All other activities were under the direct control of the Pharaoh examples of which are:
-Mining, with labor supplied by convicted criminals, prisoners of war, and slaves. The largest operations were for gold, stone, and metallic ores.
-Manufacturing, including cotton, linen and silk clothing, perfumes, beer, wine, shipbuilding, sail making and many others, some of which were operated by individuals or shared with the managers of Egypt's affairs.
-Army, with manpower recruited from the population as needed. There is no record of a permanent Army.
-Navy, records indicate that the Nile had two to three thousand ships, and the Mediterranean two hundred bireme or larger warships, two hundred trading vessels of up to two hundred tons capacity, and one hundred for coastal protection and other uses. As a consequence, in Cleopatra's time, this meant she had a force of twenty thousand Navy Marines as a permanent military force. With no functioning Canal (it was silted up), her secret was her differently designed three hundred strong trading fleet sailing between the Port of Berenike, India, and elsewhere. This fleet alone had over ten thousand Navy Marines on board.

Missing from this listing are some of the most important people in Egypt, the scribes. By tradition, they were trained by the Temples but worked in large numbers for the Pharaoh. By Queen Cleopatra the VII's time in 40 BC, these scribes kept track of every detail of Egypt's economy from Trade values to the profitability of every export product and every manufacturing and trading business in the Country. Thus, she was able to fine-tune every aspect of the economy to ensure full employment and optimum profitability, a fact that was recorded in Egyptian writings.

The economic structure (barter) that accompanied the above was a thing of simplicity and beauty. However, over the millennia and under Cleopatra and the demands of her widespread Trading organization, it began to change, and it is that system that we will describe. With bartering and trade with coinage being transacted side by side, it is the perfect way to show how that transition was handled. At the start, with theoretically all the land being owned by the Pharaoh, the people worked for three things. Raising food, making clothing, and other goods to support everyday living requirements, and protection from attack or crime. With everything being raised from the land, that was where the bartering process began. Claiming a share of everything being grown, raised, or made from those products (called the Hor Aha in 3100 BC), the bartering components were part of those crops and the animals being raised from them. To balance those exchanges, instead the promise of work was used as the way to settle any small differences. We also need to remember that the managers working for the Pharaoh were in turn allocated enough land to compensate them for their time and costs of doing that work. Later, the work of collecting their part of the barter arrangement was also passed on to them. By 2100 BC, it was further refined to include the use of Deben as a way of completing bartering deals. These Deben were known weights and purity of silver and gold ingots and used to conduct large transactions or exchanges that could not be completed by one of the sides. After 700 BC, coins were introduced, gradually replacing Deben. To complete the story of barter and its four-thousand-year history, we need to understand how its wealth was stored and spent:

-Labor owed to the Pharaohs was used to mine gold, stone, and other products, with much of it ending up in the hands of the Temples.

-Trading profits, mostly in the form of silver coinage, was stored away by Cleopatra and her trading partners.

-Buildings, Temples, and Tomb construction accounted for how most of the remaining barter was spent. In summary, under the bartering system, once the product had left the farm, no further taxes were assessed, and indeed, with further bartering would have been impossible to trace. Similarly, the same thing happened with manufactured goods. Thus, taxes were assessed and collected at the source of production with everything after that being tax-free. Egypt was operating on what we would call today a Value Added Tax system (VAT). Collecting taxes from the user was viewed as being too expensive and vulnerable to dishonesty.

$$$$$

When Caesar Augustus captured Egypt in 30 BC, he was stunned at the size of Cleopatra's treasure. However, knowing that the amount of silver coinage lost to Trade by Rome was even greater, he and his descendants kept mounting expeditions over the next two hundred years. The problem was that the most likely site was in the Faiyum area of Egypt. Unfortunately, due to constant changes in the surrounding geography, it had become lost to subsequent generations, with descriptions of its location by such people as Herodotus leading to more confusion. It was in an attempt to sort this out and learn the history of the early Canals into the Faiyum, one of which was said to have been built by Joseph of Biblical fame that started me off on this journey. And so, this is where my learning process about the basics of trade and its economics began.

$$$$$

THE MESSAGE OF THE SEVEN-YEAR DROUGHT

The lessons for us today are perhaps more urgent for us than at any time in our history. With few in the USA government seeming to understand, or have chosen to ignore, is why our food system is now in greater jeopardy from catastrophes and weather-related events than at any time in our history. Not only have we gotten rid of all our food reserves, and no longer have control over where our products are grown (our flawed Trading Policy), and so in the event of future shortages occurring, the country of origin, and not the USA, will determine our fate. How quickly we have forgotten WWII, and its lessons, not to mention the earlier dust bowl. I'm afraid I have had to add a further sentence here, for a certain government employee, who shall be nameless, retorted that we had a one year or more storage system in place, and so why do we need more? Obviously, he did not understand that with harvests only once per year, the minimum storage needed was slightly over one year, and that did not leave anything left over for emergencies. Indeed, when pressed, he did admit that dictates to reduce our national budget was what killed our safety program, and was another casualty of our Trading Policy. For our politicians, unlike the rest of we poor mortals, ignorance is bliss.

In case there are still doubters of this almost simplistic wisdom from those times, let me relate a more recent tale. The last time we had a major crop failure here in the USA was with soybeans of all things. Not a crucial crop regarding diet, but still important in some countries. At any rate, the US Government in its wisdom ordered the cut-off, of sales to Japan, to protect buyers here in the USA.

Within the year, Japan signed contracts with Brazil, setting off an explosion in land clearing, with cropland now dedicated to soybean production, an ecological disaster as the rain forest was burned down, and, as an ultimate insult, only buying small quantities from then on, from the USA. We cannot blame Japan, for their priority was the security of supply, but cutting off our biggest customer, was a move, almost as insane as eliminating the inventory of such a critical supply as food.

We should keep in storage enough food to tide us through disasters. Not just grain, but all the fruits, meats, fish and drinks we require. In the USA, we learned that lesson after the dust bowl in the twenties and thirties. WWII only emphasized that need, and expanding that program to make the USA the granary center of the world.

What happened to it? It is a sad story of greed, abuse, lying politicians, and ignorance. When one builds up reserves far more than one needs at the time, inevitably prices drop and is the free market's way to stop farmers growing more produce. Thus, to keep the reserve intact, one needs to set the price at levels that will encourage farmers to continue growing that crop. Sounds simple, so why did that not work? With guaranteed prices to the farmer, our politicians forgot that the buyer's price also had to be guaranteed. With the world and retail prices free to move at market price, the Government had to cover the difference. An expense that was deemed to be too great, and so the program was eventually phased out with the label of being a subsidy to the farmer prevailing, and something that was a complete distortion of the facts. The answer was simplicity itself; make it applicable to domestic production only.

We now come to the situation today. Since 1900, our world population has quintupled. Many of our supplies are no longer 'home grown,' and come from distant lands, some of which are not friendly. We have introduced new software called 'Just-In-Time' inventory control. (Computers now order supplies to meet requirements that are needed only immediately, saving the seller, and distributor money, by reducing inventory and spoilage at every level). Have you ever noticed how grocery stores quickly empty in less than twenty-four hours whenever poor weather threatens? Just think what might happen if something serious occurred. When disaster inevitably happens, it will be too late to prevent starvation, and God preserves us, from the horrors that typically follow.

$$$$$

THE MESSAGE OF THE BARTER SYSTEM

Any system of values has its limitations, especially in times of difficulty. Inevitably, to survive, it has to be linked or related to something of known value (Base Product). If not, then that very system will, in turn, begin to fluctuate with its own perceived worth. If we follow Joseph's genius, that should not be confused with the worth of that 'Base Product,' changing. For if that happens, the system's values move up or down in concert with the 'Base Product,' and yet, at the same time, allow barter values, between products, the freedom to change as conditions change, a double thinking type of relationship.

As Trade became international, coupled with long periods to complete barter transactions, barter increasingly began to be replaced, with what the Egyptians had called gold or silver Debens, but were now being called coins. By Cleopatra's time, the world's mightiest Empire, Rome, had decided to use silver coinage, as its base currency, with gold only used for very large transactions.

If one thinks about it, the size of their economy was now dependent on the amount of gold and silver they had on hand. Unable to grow beyond that amount, they adopted the expedient of going to war and capturing more gold and silver from the defeated, thus freeing the way for their economy to further expand.

There was only one problem. When Cleopatra cornered the Trading Market between Asia and Rome, and they had nothing of value to offer in return, they inevitably ended up by paying for these imports with silver coinage. By 30 BC, Rome had run out of silver with Caesar Augustus left with no choice but to invade Egypt and steal back that silver coinage, and that is what happened. We are not done yet from that lesson, for over the following centuries, Rome, with a growing economy and fewer countries left to invade, kept running out of silver for the coinage to allow that growth. Debasement, devaluation, inflation, and bankruptcy haunted that system proving once and for all that it was patently ridiculous to tie the size of one's economy or to limit its growth to a product such as silver or gold. What then would Joseph's solution have been?

He would have done what we do today, issue fiat currency, of no value in itself, but tied to faith in the issuer of that same currency. If the issuer plays games with that currency such that the users lose faith in it, and it loses value, so be it. It is their fault, and it should be allowed to fail. The problem comes if it is one of the supporting currencies for a world system. To that extent, so all world systems will rise and fall to the same degree as that percentage changes.

Unfortunately, in the real world, markets over or undershoot what should have been arithmetic value calculations. So, what would he have done next? He would have stopped those games. And as they say in my Church, 'Here endeth the Lesson.' It is not the currency that is at fault it is the manipulator!

$$$$$

CLEOPATRA

Appreciated by few was the brilliance of this woman and how she single-handedly made Egypt the 'Trading Giant' of its time. In turn, that achievement made Egypt the wealthiest Nation under Roman influence. Initially, when she became Queen, Egypt was still an independent Country, but under Rome's protection and given the mostly meaningless Title of 'Friend and Ally of Rome.' With other countries, such as Greece, having been conquered by Rome, they were called Provinces and ruled by Roman 'Governors'. Cleopatra thus took great pains to try and preserve her country's 'status quo' with Rome. After Julius Caesar landed in Alexandria and with his Legions, defeated and killed her brother, rather than appointing a Governor and leaving it as just another Province, he appointed a Tribune, with three Legions to keep an eye on Cleopatra. The why of this by Romantic novelists was the fact that she had become his mistress and bore him a son. The reality was stark. She had paid back a huge loan Caesar had given her father. Also, she had supported Caesar with a fleet of one hundred bireme ships, allowing him to rush to the defense of the Province of Roman Asia (Turkey) from rebel invaders. On balance, he had doubtless recognized her brilliance and ability to manage Egypt as a friend and ally. On Cleopatra's part, she was more than happy with this arrangement, determining that she would somehow have to remain close to whoever ruled Rome. Unluckily for her, Caesar was assassinated with his drunken successor unable to protect Cleopatra at the end.

Cleopatra's one mistake was not to know when to stop. Over the next twenty years of her reign, she accumulated such a positive trading balance with Rome that she ended up with nearly all of Rome's silver coinage, leaving Rome with the choice of either going bankrupt or attacking and taking back that coinage by force. For Rome, the choice was simple, and for Cleopatra tragic. So, what can we learn from that Lady?

First and foremost, to keep detailed records of what was going on in Trade. Not just cash flow, but profitability by industry and individual businesses, for that, is how you make the most money, and at the same time make sure your people and their jobs are kept both safe and prosperous.

Second, control your transportation system. She oversaw the building of the world's most advanced technological fleet such that it remained the standard of excellence for the next 1,500 years. Not satisfied with just that, she made sure of its longevity and loyalty by making sure her trading partners shared in its ownership. For, once a partner and sharing in the fleet's profits, the trading partners would want to ensure their partnership continued! In other words, she also dominated the Service side of Trade.

Third, she made sure that even with such a mundane staple as wheat, that barter was done as much as possible (Balanced trade). On the other hand, there was no question that she made sure that the high valued product was at the heart of the business. In her case silk, spices, herbs, and gemstones. (In Rome, silk was stated to be worth its weight in gold).

Lastly, communications between the trading partners were superb with meticulous attention being paid to record keeping, for trust was everything.

The contrast between Rome (the loser) and Egypt (the winner) could not have been clearer and what led us to compare the two with what is going on today. Namely, between the USA, (the loser) and China, Germany, Japan, and S. Korea, (the winners).

The flaw was the same as for the USA today. If she had kept track of the cumulative trade numbers, she would have known when Rome was in trouble and been ready to cut back trade or spend some of it in Rome, possibly by the simple expedient of lending them the money.

$$$$$

ROME

We return now to history, replete with hundreds of examples of bankruptcies, some involving Cleopatra and Rome.

Julius Caesar, after his victory over Gaul, returned to Rome only to find that his political opponents had already fled, but not before emptying the treasury of all Coinage, removing the staff, and the Mint closed. Rome's whole financial system was based on silver, and so, until he could convert his vast silver booty captured in Gaul into coinage, he was without funds to pay his troops. Left with only promises, he was forced to double the amounts he promised to pay his troops telling them that once he defeated their enemy, they would at long last be paid. However, after his victory at the Battle of Pharsalus, Pompey had fled with his war chests to Egypt. With most of his own Army in open revolt over being unpaid, he ordered Mark Antony to march them back to Rome where he would catch up with them and settle all debts later. Gathering a rag-tag mixture of Pompey's legionaries that had surrendered to him, he had then boarded some of Pompey's captured ships and chased after him. Unfortunately for him, Pompey had been murdered, and his surviving wife and children were already on their way to NW Africa, complete with the missing war chests. Demanding payment of the four thousand Talents of silver that was his half of the loan he and Pompey had earlier loaned to the previous Pharaoh, the boy-Pharaoh, and his advisors declined payment. Thus, started the 'Alexandrian War.' While not documented in Caesar's Diaries, what happened next was fairly obvious. After his victory and the death of the boy-Pharaoh, he found Cleopatra to be the only person who could give him the money he so desperately needed. Thus, he had reappointed her Queen and traveled up the Nile to Thebes where Egypt's Royal Treasury was located. Once paid, Caesar was free to travel back to Rome, which, after a diversion to settle an uprising, he duly did.

With this as the background, he arrived in Rome to find it in chaos. Mark Antony, far from looking after things, had been on one of his several month's long alcoholic binges. With little coinage, Rome was in the classic position of too little currency chasing too few goods with a deflationary recession in full swing. What happened next was pure Julius Caesar. First, he reopened the Mint and ordered that they commence converting his vast booty from Gaul into silver coinage. Second, he ordered that the importation of luxury goods be prohibited until further notice, for he had learned first-hand from Cleopatra about her trading success. Next, with the funds paid to him by Cleopatra, he paid his troops and other debts, and with what remained, commenced a huge reconstruction program for Rome, including a revamping of its water supplies and bathing facilities. What most do not know is that of all the job creators, construction is the greatest with the factor today being a multiplier of ten. In Rome's day and without machinery, probably three times that. His genius was what he did next. Appreciating that with most of Rome's citizens were still weighed down by debt, and what he had done so far would not be sufficient to get their economy back to normal, he ordered that all interest charges on loans be forgiven. However, the original amount of the loan would still have to be repaid. Analysts have estimated that this move would have reduced Rome's debts by 75% overnight, for the economy returned to normal within the year. His genius was also in the fact that by ordering that the principle is paid back, faith in Rome's economy was preserved while still ending the recession of 46 BC.

By 31 BC, Rome's economy was again in trouble. This time it was a different problem, with its then leader, Julius Caesar's nephew Octavian, later to be renamed Caesar Augustus, for it was running out of coins and threatening Rome with a new recession, this one again deflationary, but from a different cause, too many imports! With having little to barter, Rome had been paying for their imports with their silver coinage, and in turn, Egypt was paying Asia in gold. Thus, Egypt was soon amassing huge piles of silver coinage. This was a target Rome could not ignore, with Octavian invading Egypt in 30 BC. With Rome's Senate under his control, Octavian persuaded them to name Egypt as having been captured by him and not Rome, thus Egypt becoming his personal property, and not as usual to be just another Province of Rome. Like his Uncle before him, Octavian went on a building spree with Rome's economy soon back to normal, but this time with himself holding the purse strings. Interestingly, the above arrangement survived, and was passed on to the now infamous Emperors Caligula and Nero, whose funds from their ownership of Egypt allowed them to become independent from their Senate, and openly, the Dictators of Rome.

So, what can we learn from these lessons? As long as the currency is supported by something trustworthy such as silver or gold, it is invulnerable to inflation. On the other hand, if these commodities become scarce, then deflation becomes the problem. The answer is paper or base metal currency ('Fiat Currency'), providing it is in turn backed up by trust in the issuer of that currency. If that trust comes into question, then that currency will, in turn, become vulnerable to inflation, dependent on the degree of distrust at that time. The other lesson is that if trade becomes out of balance and is carried to extremes, a nation's economy can become a casualty leading to chaos and economic turmoil. In the case of a currency that is also the reserve currency for all others, then they too all become equally vulnerable to those inflationary pressures, but this time dependent on their trading balances.

$$$$$

EUROPEAN COLONIALISM

No matter how innocent sounding the word might be, it did not mask the fact that it was still the old attack and conquest of ancient times. Ranging from brutal occupation to benign and peaceful settlement, virtually all Colonies have since been granted their independence. Almost unnoticed in this process of abandonment was the fact that no one seemed to recognize the importance of Trade to these emerging Nations. Or, perhaps, the departing occupier wanted to maintain their trading profits with that country for as long as possible. In any event, no matter the reason, only with trading skills, can a new nation survive else it inevitably disintegrates into chaos and bankruptcy. The examples of these stories are so numerous that to me the above should be considered a truism. And here I do not include raw material mining operations owned by outsiders, for they hardly qualify as having passed on trading skills to the local people.

COUNTRY/TIMIN G	WEALTH SOURCES	FAILURE CAUSE
Persia 3000-2000 BC	Farming/Trade/Conquest	Land poisoning/Defeat
Egypt 2000-300 BC	Farming/Gold/Conquest	Incestuous marriages
Greece 300-150 BC	Trade/Conquest	Corruption/Defeat
Rome 150-50 BC	Trade/Conquest	Corruption/Silver coins
Egypt 55-30 BC	Trade/Navy	No Army
Rome 30 BC-650 AD	Conquest/Colonization	Fiscal Policy, Silver, Defeat
Muslims 650-950 AD	Conquest/Colonization	Corruption/Defeat
France 950-1150 AD	Conquest/Colonization	Corruption/Defeat
Spain/Portugal 1500-1600	Conquest/Colonization	Naval Defeat
Holland 1650-1700	Colonization/Trade	Naval Defeat
UK 1700-1939	Colonization/Trade	War Cost/Policy/Trade
USA 1939-1990	Trade/Farming/Minerals/Oil	Policy/Trade/Inaction
Japan 1960-1980	Manufacturing/Trade	Fiscal Policy
Germany 1980-2017	Trade/Import Barriers	
China 2005-2017	Manufacturing/Trade Barriers	

COUNTRY DOMINANCE/TIMING AND TRADE BALANCE

As a rough guide, I have listed the main European Countries involved in this Colonization process. Please note that rather than worry about the exact dates of transition, for many of these took many years to occur, the important thing was the sequence, and what happened during the periods of change that followed. After losing coinage dominance, within a few years those nations could no longer afford standing armies, and so lost their position of World dominance and leadership to those that followed, often involving wars and rebellions, for most did not like giving up their leadership. In nearly half the cases, war and defeat were the final ends to their dominance. However, most were preceded by neglect of Trade, which in turn led to the demise of Trading dominance and wealth. Some stranger reasons were, in the case of Persia, the poisoning of the land from irrigation without drainage, and in Egypt, the bizarre case of incestuous marriages.

Of the hundreds of indicators that attempt to read and forecast economic performance, we found none that comes even close to that which measures the cumulative Positive or Negative Balance of Trade. Tested against over three thousand years of history, it is also the only predictor of which countries will become the future power centers and leaders of this World. With cash flowing in, money can be spent to increase everything from living conditions to military might, and with that comes prestige and admiration, followed soon after by Leadership. Conversely, if cash is flowing out, debt is the only stopgap, chased soon after by the printing of money or debasement, which may delay the moment of truth, but the result always remains bankruptcy. Something that does not inspire thoughts of Leadership.

Any economists worth their salt will tell you 'Cash is King', and so it is with this method of measuring success or failure. However, the listing does not quantify the status of each country, either the standard of living or its status as a civilized society. In other words, how and on what it has spent its resources to that point, which perhaps explains some of the surprises in our list, but then, history is full of them, and hence the caution, or should I say warning? The second is size. As an example, Singapore has made the 'Very Strong' list yet is so small a nation it cannot be considered a candidate for leadership. With no military, it must become an increasingly attractive target for its neighbors. Thirdly, if wealthy and powerful from past glories, yet losing cash, the transition can be both long and painful, for the fall is even steeper, as was the case with ancient Greece. Lastly, the character of people is also not a part of this equation.

The top ten Countries with trade surpluses all share one secret in common. They have made exporting to their countries a difficult undertaking with a combination of regulations, standards, approval requirements, currency exchange restrictions, tariffs, Government mandates, and manipulation of VAT and Sales Taxes to replace income taxes as a way to penalize the would-be exporter to their Country.

Some obvious comments about this listing and World Leadership need to be made. Small Countries with few military forces such as Singapore, do not qualify as a candidate due to their inability to enforce decisions. On the other hand, countries such as Switzerland gain admiration and respect for their achievements.

$$$$$

CHAPTER III

MODERN TRADE

The world's current trading balance by country shows who are the winners and losers in today's battle for dominance.

2016 WORLD TRADE RANKING*
(All data from CIA in Billion US $)

VERY LARGE	LARGE	LARGE	VERY LARGE
271 China	26 Norway	-19 Libya	-470 USA
301 Germany	29 Thailand	-17 Iraq	-157 UK
176 Japan	26 Sweden	-14 Columbia	-57 Canada
102 S. Korea	20 Denmark	-14 Brazil	-44 Australia
70 Netherlands	24 Spain	-13 Argentina	-42 Saudi Arabia
78 Taiwan	4 Kuwait**	-13 Oman	-32 Turkey
61 Switzerland	4 UAE**	-13 Egypt	-32 India
39 Russia	10 Austria	-12 France	-29 Mexico
57 Singapore	10 Israel	-12 Venezuela	-25 Algeria
40 Italy	17 Iran	-11 Lebanon	-21 Indonesia

TRADE SURPLUS   **TRADE DEFICIT**

*The listing is in the order for 2015, but the numbers are from 2016.

** Reflects a one year price drop in oil?

The numbers, in fact, should have been calculated to show the trade imbalance since 1975, but with none of the individual nation's numbers being available on that basis, it would have been a herculean task, and too time-consuming. However, I can tell you that at least over the last ten years our story holds true.

It would be hard not to compare world trade among Nations with a modern shopping mall. The analogy would be that each store was like a Nation and that its cash flow and profit or loss was like that of a Nation's economic health. The philosophical question would then arise that if there were only one big shop (or

Nation), would the cash flow then automatically be in the balance and so not matter? The answer is no, for the difference would be equal to the profit or loss being made. Thus, when measuring whether or not a Country has a positive or negative balance of trade, it tells us two things. First, it tells us whether that country's currency is strengthening or weakening. After that, only that Country can tell itself whether or not that business was profitable. Then, and only then, can it be determined whether or not that country can sustain its trading position, with time always the true determinate of that fact. And that, everyone, is why the cumulative balance of Trade, over several years, is so crucial to know, when trying to assess a Nation's long-term economic health.

In other words, cash flow, which is the trade balance, is important when measuring the status of a country's currency. It is the implied profit or loss behind that number that is the issue when attempting to measure the financial health of a Nation. At this point discussion inevitably becomes one of what type of business is the main contributor to profits. History tells us it can be many things from creative art to wheat or whatever other people need. It does not matter what the product is. The issue is that it is needed and to become wealthy, all that has to happen is the seller or trader has to sell more of it than the other party is exporting. The point being we have come full circle back to the premise that a positive balance of trade is the key measurement of a country's financial health, but of far more importance is the gaining or losing of capital.

Using this measurement, I focused on three Countries, in particular, having lived in each of them for many years. They were the United Kingdom, Canada, and the USA. Each of them had the same symptoms. Trade deficits over many years; a consequent difficulty in balancing their domestic budgets; a loss of domestic manufacturing as they increasingly relied on imports for their basic needs; finding jobs for their own people; being forced to print money in order to avoid bankruptcy; and lastly, a loss of leadership and relevance as their money supply and power dwindled.

$$$$$

THE UK

The story with Great Britain was the easiest to decipher. Two World Wars and its colossal financial burden on a small country was what did it. Years of building their Empire and maritime dominance was gradually lost, with the dissolution of its Empire the price for USA Aid in the second World War. Domestic Manufacturing and Trade, which had always been their strength, was neglected in favor of social programs after the war, and further compounded by the

USA's Marshall Plan, which provided capital to Germany, Austria, Italy and Japan to replace their destroyed factories with modern ones. We then saw the incredible fiasco of the winner losing out to the defeated regarding manufacturing efficiency. Many years later, that fiasco is still being felt.

Unfortunately for the UK, the discovery of North Sea oil masked the early stages of this trend, and it was not until 1998 as oil exports started a long decline that the trade problem started to rear its head. From then until 2016 that cumulative deficit reached $1 trillion, with 2016 reaching $0.06 trillion in one year of trade. While that pales into insignificance compared to the USA's imbalance of $0.47 trillion, as a percent of GDI, both are close to 15% and thus very much faced with the same problem. However, with 'Brexit' looming, the UK's imbalance problem might be solved, but only if imports, mostly from Germany, and currently worth some $100 billion per year, are replaced with domestically produced products in the UK.

In the process, with the UK's Service Industry offering the USA access to the Euromarkets, both are now exposed to that being shut off to them.

Regarding forming new Trade partnerships, the quickest way for the UK to do this is by making trading alliances with their friends, with the ancient one of shared language probably holding out the most promise. Conversely, the quickest way to fail would be to split up into their original four Kingdoms, with each becoming less significant in terms of world leadership. It would indeed be a sad ending for a nation that has played such a significant role in shaping our modern world.

$$$$$

CANADA

The tale of Canada I find even sadder, for its potential is perhaps one of the greatest in the world. Blessed with natural resources, vast farmlands, and scenic beauty, it is a land that should be the richest in the world. What happened? It was a land that though independent, could not stop copying and responding to the needs of its neighbor to the south. Indeed, every indication is that it still does not realize what has happened, for domestic manufacturing and exports are still being neglected as imports continue to pour into their country. Despite this, and due to the fact of its wealth of natural resources, Canada has been able to run a positive balance of trade since 1975 though having increasing problems in doing so since 2009. As a consequence, its debt clock has started to creep upwards with it now reaching into the six-billion-dollar range last year. The solution to their problem is the same as for the USA, and Australia, but not nearly as severe.

$$$$$

AUSTRALIA

On the surface Australia looks like it is in a healthy economic situation regarding trade, with the recent string of negative trade balances due to some reductions in China, Japan, and S. Korea's raw material needs, and in turn, their exports of finished products to the USA.

Longer term, one of two things is going to happen. The USA fixes its trade problem, in which case their imports from all three of those Countries will decline. Hopefully Australia can switch some of its raw material exports to the USA as their own needs increase, but that is far from certain. The other situation is if the USA does not fix its trade problem, then they will enter a long period of economic decline and turmoil with their economy in crisis, something that will impact China, Japan, and S. Korea equally. In other words, either way the outlook for these three Countries is equally grim if the USA does not fix its trading debacle.

While Australia's current trade deficit balances don't look huge when compared to the USA's, those drains on cash flowing out of the Country to buy imports are serious given the relatively small population. Somehow, Australia has to find a way to encourage the formation of small domestic consumer industries. In that endeavor, mandating domestic sources to supply infrastructure needs and security needs is one way that will not raise objections from trading partners for they too do the same in their home Country. Likewise, if to reduce fossil fuel use, that might encourage many industries to become established or set up production facilities in Australia.

$$$$$

THE EXPORTERS

CHINA

It goes without saying that China historically has been a one-way trader in that it had a centrally controlled economy denying any imports with the sole exception being products they could not mine or manufacture themselves. Even today, with many of those earlier restrictions lifted, anything deemed to be for their military or involving China's security is still banned. In the meantime, the outright theft of technology, patents, and copyright continues unabated with would be sellers into that market being forced to give up their manufacturing secrets and technology as the price of entry. The words 'Free Trade' are a joke when applied to this country with the USA being held in nothing but contempt.

The trade data more than bears that out and with significant trade only starting in 2002, the cumulative trade data since then shows something extraordinary and completely idiotic that jumps out of from that data:

2002-2016 CHINA CUMULATIVE TRADE STATISTICS
(US$ trillions)

	EXPORTS	IMPORTS	BALANCE
WORLD	21.536	18.089	3.447
USA	5.000	1.166	3.834
All Others	16.536	16.923	-0.387

(USDC and WITS data).

If we can believe it, China's trade balance with the rest of the world is negative. Only the United States numbers jump out showing the insanity and ignorance of our leaders to what has been happening for their cumulative balance of trade with the USA have reached the staggering number of over $3.8 trillion since 2002. That means that $3.8 trillion has left our Country and has been injected into the Chinese economy as capital and all by itself has financed China's growth. Talk about being asleep that does not even begin to describe it. This is shear madness carried to extremes which border on the criminal. I even went back over the data to double check the numbers, but what they were saying was the USA had virtually been alone in letting trade with China getting out of control. Can our dense leaders now begin to understand what our President was threating to do against China: literally to stop the bandwagon, stop further growth, but not only that, nip in the bud its grandiose plans for world leadership?

An evil thought now arose in my mind. With N. Korea a lackey and the only fellow Communist State in Asia, how could China distract the USA's attention away from trade? I leave that to your imagination. In the meantime, sitting down with China and correcting the situation gradually would be appropriate for none of our politicians or leaders seem to have understood what was happening, and sadly what it meant.

How the Chinese must despise us for our ignorance with even my Chinese and Korean golfing buddies laughing at the stupidity of our leaders and politicians. The one thing I learned from working in Asia was the brilliance of its people, and coupled with their work ethic a formidable force with which to be reckoned. Not for one minute should we think they do not already understand what has been happening and in fact are way ahead of us in their long-term planning and maneuvering for the future, for the tell-tale signs are everywhere. As an example, under normal conditions, a country such as China with huge positive balances of trade for the last fourteen years would have had to battle rising pressures to raise the value of their currency. However, by increasing borrowing (US $4.6 trillion) to allow an increasing amount of investment, it has managed so far to offset that problem, a brilliant move with much of that focus directed towards the gaining of world leadership from the USA. Make no mistake, China plays for keeps and if some of its strategies pose risks, so be it.

One last thought, would you have liked to have seen some of the things China has done happening in the USA as well? If so, you now know the answer, but even sadder, we only have ourselves to blame.

$$$$$

GERMANY

If there were ever a country that deliberately constructed barriers to imported products, Germany would have won first prize. Regarding Trade surplus, Germany is now number one in the world and with it has come wealth and prosperity to the point it has relegated the rest of the Euro-market countries to second-class citizenship. How did it do this? For that story, we need to go back to the nineteen thirties under Nazi Germany and how Adolph Hitler laid the groundwork for their success today. We forget how clever was this evil genius. Devious and devoid of ethics or morals, the system he left behind was designed only to allow goods to be imported that suited Germany, and after WW II was still intact. In the 1920's and 1930's, Hitler could see that the Treaty of Versailles had left Germany in economic shambles. With no money left in Germany after making reparations, and access denied to world capital resources, and unemployment everywhere, the only way left was to raise capital by exporting products overseas and to use that incoming cash to rebuild his Country. In speeches, he bluntly told the people of Germany it was going to be a case of export or perish. Introducing an incredibly complicated system of Unions, Craft Guilds, Standards, Specifications, and Approval Procedures to limit imports to the bare minimum, that was the system still in place when the Second World War ended. With the bureaucracy relatively unchanged, that, in turn, became the system inherited by modern Germany.

Again, after WW II, with its economy and country in shambles, this time it did have a trading system in place. While unfair, in terms of the ideal of 'Free Trade,' it was one of the few ways by which Germany could once again raise capital and with the help of the USA's Marshall Plan rebuild its exporting Industries.

As a consequence, if one wants to export into Germany, you may have to wait up to ten years to gain clearance and approval, find a mandated partner for that process, which by then, the average seller would have long ago given up on that effort. In other words, the inherited system from the 1930's has been deliberately left intact creating the barrier to imports we find today. Indeed, while little known, several other European Countries have adopted some of these same techniques including one that if you close or shut down a business, you have to pay the employees for the rest of their lives! Thus, reliance on such things as import duties to protect their domestic industries has proven to be unnecessary.

Since 1975, while the USA was in the process of losing $18 trillion to trade, illegal drugs and war, Germany was tucking away $3 trillion by trade alone which they used as a capital infusion to improve their economy. Normally, under those circumstances, a nation's currency would increase in value offsetting some of those gains. However, with Germany using Euro currency, that did not happen and as it turned out for Germany a fortuitous decision.

Another example is how the USA got further 'snookered' by the ECU. In the USA, there is no Value Added Tax (VAT), but rather a sales tax that goes directly to the individual State tax collectors. The Federal Government relies on Income taxes for the bulk of its income. In Europe, the average VAT tax is currently 19% with the revenue raised going directly to the country in which it is taxed. Only then is a small portion remitted to the Common Market. In other words, it is a major part of the income for each European Country with income taxes correspondingly reduced. Take a guess what taxes importers have to pay? All applicable duties plus a 19% VAT tax supposedly to offset what European producers have to pay, but in essence paying some of their income taxes!

As for Switzerland, they have proven to be the past masters of the service industries. So, how does one fight this system? One either copies it or forms a group more to one's liking.

$$$$

JAPAN, S. KOREA, SINGAPORE, AND TAIWAN.

Nothing happens in those Countries without their Government's (in consultation with interested parties), approval.   End of discussion. The only question is why the USA still is allowing it to happen for all of them long ago recovered from the ashes of WWII.

$$$$$

CHAPTER IV

CREATING WEALTH

Let's assume for the moment that our World is one civilization with no countries or regional alliances, currencies, or other barriers to divide it into sub-units. Any attempts to gain or lose wealth would be between individuals with no restraints as to how much could be amassed. The only constraint to such changes would be socio-economic ones that would define how the wealth was being created and spent and the degree to which it was being accumulated by groups or individuals versus being spent on improvements to the World in general. Rather than being distracted by such considerations and to allow us to focus on economic fundamentals, let's further imagine that we have a Government in place that has superimposed a set of rules to assure an equitable system of taxes and disbursements to spread incomes in an acceptable way to all its citizens.

Existing wealth might be defined as all artistic works of art, precious metals and jewels, fixed assets, production facilities, infrastructure not included as fixed assets, and money on hand (M1 to M4). While one could debate that the value of education and training should be included, that does not change what follows.

Having settled on that number, let's address the sole issue of what changes that number. Obvious would be the fact that plus or minus changes to everything on our list should automatically be factored in. What else could there be? I submit nothing.

There is however another factor and that is fiat currency. That needs to be raised or lowered as the value of GNP changes in response to the above. Is there anything else? I submit nothing. If there is please let me know.

$$$$$

Now, let's return to how our World is today. I know it's a bit of a jolt for everything now becomes complicated. First, we have barriers of different kinds between the countries which include natural, trade, cultural, racial, currency, and probably others, the most common of which is war or antagonism. In terms of the impact on economics, only three are of importance; trade, currency, and war.

Trade, because it involves the payment of currency for imports, implies an automatic reduction in that same amount of cash in the importing country and its transfer to the exporting country. It is therefore the addition of capital to the exporter and the loss of capital to the importer. Believe it or not, something that apparently few people understand.

Currency transfers if continued without restraint for a number of years will in turn result in some dire consequences unless adjusted. For the importer, their domestic supply of currency will decline resulting in less currency chasing the same amount of domestic goods and causing deflation and an economic recession. Printing or borrowing are the two common ways to solve this problem with both having their own adverse consequence: the former resulting in inflation, and the latter, because of the cost of interest, forcing the reduction of Government Budgets in other areas if they are to remain balanced.

War has been one of the most popular choices through history for the capturing of countries leads to the capture of material goods, precious items, and free labor in the form of slavery. In modern times that option has largely been removed, for Armageddon in the form of nuclear war, has blocked that option, again something that few seem to have realized.

I think it is safe to say that to create wealth in our modern World, Trade is the only civilized mechanism left to Nations. The second truism is that if Nations have trade losses over a number of years the adverse results can become catastrophic. Under those conditions, and if counteracting these losses of currency by borrowing, then one day will eventually reach their credit limit. The other choice; to print money, will also eventually cause chaos and inflation. There is only one solution, to adjust one's economy so as to become an exporter.

While not strictly a Trade issue, there is another consequence of running continuous trade deficits. One's own manufacturing industries inevitably fall into decline with job losses meaning more people looking for work, in turn driving down wages, which in turn reduces Government tax revenue and income. In addition, the unemployed need some form of unemployment insurance or welfare to cover their living expenses thus adding to Government expenditures. With income down and expenses up, difficulties in balancing budgets also ensue with visits to lenders or the printing of money the only solutions. Again, something that few people have grasped. Indeed, they have also not understood the failure in trade has led to the failure in being able to balance budgets with both going to the same trough for rescue. If ever there was, this is the definition of a double whammy!

Another aspect of the above is what happens to the workforce when unemployment, whether acknowledged or not, lasts for long periods of time.

For that answer, I have taken the liberty of extracting some conclusions made by Nick Hanauer, that he wrote about in Politico magazine some three years ago, but are still relevant today. Using IRS data on taxation, he made the following observations:

-Over the last 40-50 years corporate profits have increased from 6% to 11% of USA Gross National Product (GNP and in Europe GNI).

-Personal reportable income meanwhile decreased from 52% to 46% of GNP.

-The truly startling figure though was that the top 1% of earners income increased from 8.5% to 22.5%. A $1.0 trillion shift from the middle and low-income groups to the wealthiest in our country. Even worse though is what has been happening over the last few years. That shift has been escalating and is currently changing by $1.5 trillion every year. In other words, with total wages flat according to the IRS, the income of the work force is now shrinking by that much while the 1% elite's is rising by that same $1.5 trillion. His bottom line is that if this continues unchecked, so unrest, discontent, and an outright return to a pitchfork solution will result. What that gentleman did not appreciate was the root cause of all of this was a negative balance of trade with at the same time high end jobs disappearing with only the lower paying ones remaining. Regardless, his thesis highlighted the fact this cannot continue without unrest and rebellion rearing its head.

Some years ago, the current US Supreme Court made a ruling that I regard as one of the worst it has ever made in terms of its unintended consequences. It basically said that the rights of a corporation were the same as for an individual in that they could henceforth make unlimited contributions to politicians when running for office. I ask you, how on earth could you compare a $100 contribution with say a $50,000,000 one? And then, using the front of a so-called Trust, the recipients were not even paying taxes on that contribution. Then, on top of that comes our 1% Elite group with million dollars plus donations to garner support for their beliefs. What followed was the creation of 'The Swamp' in Washington with the buying of votes distorting our so-called democracy into something that none of our founding fathers would have been able to recognize.

Was this the reason why answers to questions have been so difficult to find? The answer is a resounding Yes. And so next came the why? In all likelihood, not something done deliberately, but rather done to not frighten us by disclosing just how dangerous things were becoming. Everyone was obviously having difficulty with the sheer size and direction of the debt issue into which we were heading, with the longer the delay, the worse it was becoming.

Nobody disputes the fact that borrowing at some time has to stop else currency will become worthless. The debate centers around the amount or size and the timing. Hint, Rome hit problems almost at where we are now. The only difference is that Rome was not part of a world currency system, and so in that respect, we are in fresh territory. However, and this is where people who make such generalized statements are tripped up. Rome was the World!

Regardless, if not handled by our leaders, the debt issue is threatening to become so large it could become impossible to solve. However, the ultimate problem is not that. It is how we can return the USA to a wealth creating environment, and for that we have to do two things; solve the trade problem and change taxes so the wealthy are taxed at rates sufficient to offset the shift of money from US workers to the 1% Elite.

With respect to timing, I believe we are fast running out of that luxury for another element is raising its head; our retail marketing system. With the financial squeeze on our middle and working classes increasing by the minute, the switch from retail shopping to on-line is resulting in an ever-quickening pace of store closures, job losses, with a switch to on-line only speeding up more imports of lower cost goods to users. The urgency of this is something that we ignore at our peril, for retail marketing is one of the life-bloods of our country, and if decimated will have dire consequences for everyone in all walks of life from Federal, State, City, Town, and Village Tax Bases, although that last category has already been annihilated by the Walmart's of our World, and to the millions of people employed by this industry.

$$$$$

CHAPTER V

USA AND TRADE

The USA has traditionally been a Country of immigrants fleeing from persecution discrimination and overpopulation in their homelands, with truth, freedom of expression and liberty its mantra and the appeal of the above compelling. Generosity too comes with this interpretation and the allowing of time to narrow differences with their gradual disappearance the hope.

Having gone through two World Wars and since then several others, all in the name of liberating people from tyrants, the USA opened its arms to the idea of 'Free Trade' as a way of bringing wealth and improved living conditions to the emerging and poorer nations of this World. Indeed, some of our leaders even talked about wanting to 'level the playing field' between nations, again a somewhat idealistic notion.

With this as a background, I next asked myself who were the experts on this vital subject, and it turned out to be our economists. In fact, the Dictionary's definition of an Economist is one who studies Trade. That description must have been written many years ago. In modern times, with the profligate spending by our politicians in an effort to 'buy' the votes of our citizens, the pressure on our currency has been increasing to the point the economists are almost running out of games they can play to support it. The politicians in the meantime have resorted to 'kicking the can down the road,' leaving some nameless person to clean up their mess. Guess who that is? 'We have met the enemy, and it is us! Most of our economists are now employed trying to think up ways of saving and rescuing our currency, our debt obligations, and our economy. Obviously, with that task, they were far too busy to keep their eye on such a dull subject as Trade.

Next turning to the US Department of commerce, I found the yearly and monthly data meticulously recorded in about every possible way one could wish. But wait, there was no cumulative date that could tell me where we stood. Digging deeper, I found the data went back on a yearly basis further than I was interested, but still nothing on a beginning or ending balance. In other words, it is like looking at a monthly Bank Statement, but without the beginning or ending balances. Just how stupid did our civil servants and politicians think we are? The sad part is that no one seems to be complaining and so we evidently are!

Reality is like taking a cold shower in the morning, quickly and unabashedly waking us to our surroundings but never-the-less enervating. In that process, the sudden or eye-catching things are what get our attention with the gradual and insidious remaining unnoticed.

The first shock was finding out that the last time the USA had a positive balance of trade, including services, was 1975, or 42 years ago! While the USA publishes information on our yearly balance of payments, nothing appears or is mentioned about the cumulative number. Regardless, I spent a month digging out the records for the last 42 years and then adding them up. Whatever the total was, we knew it should match our cumulative debt number, for at least the Treasury Dept. tries to match the printing of additional money to the growth in GNP. Thus, the printing of money was not how those cash flows out of our Country was covered but left borrowing as the source. From looking at the individual years, I sensed that the numbers would be large but surely not unmanageable. Stunned, shocked, obscene were the words that came to mind. How could anyone in their right mind have allowed this to happen? Now I was beginning to understand why these numbers had never been published for they would have caused an uproar from even the most disinterested of our people.

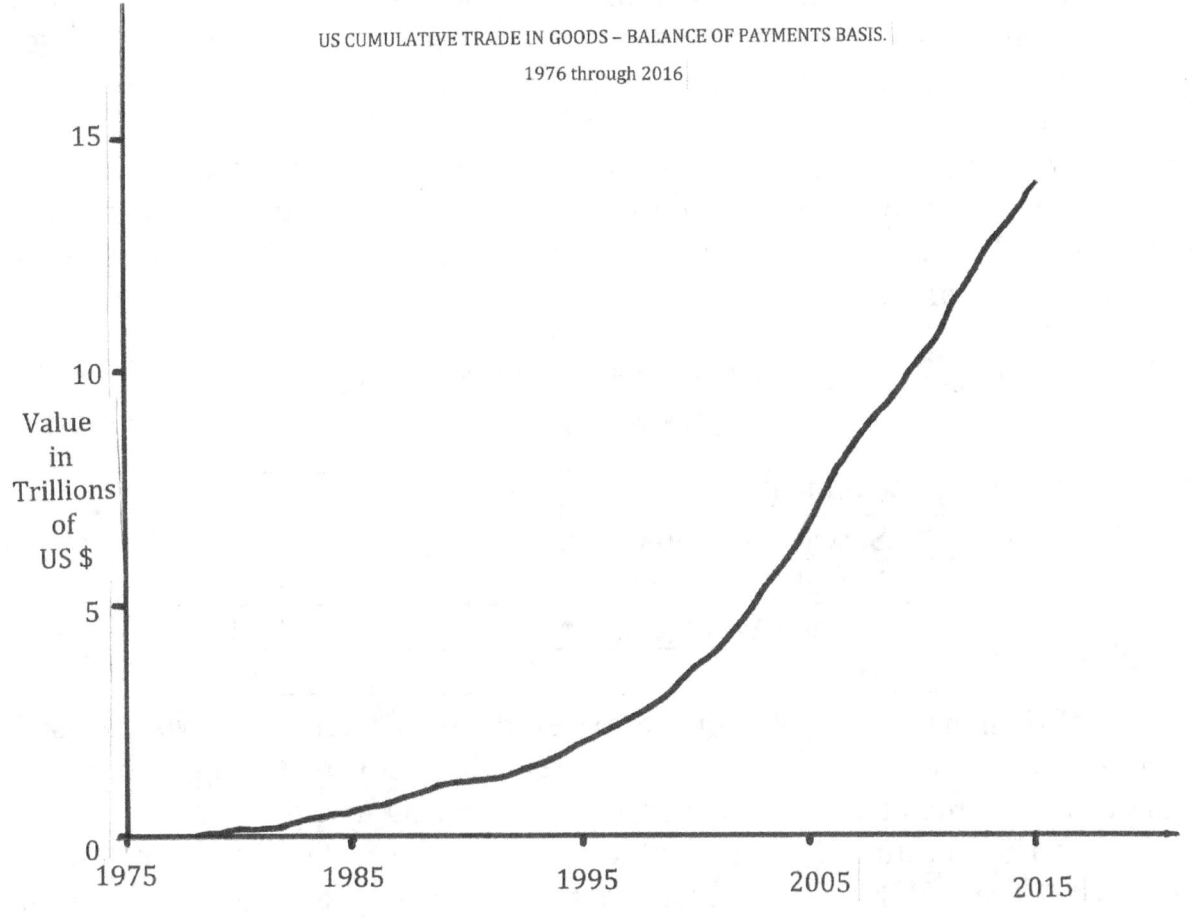

US CUMULATIVE TRADE IN GOODS – BALANCE OF PAYMENTS BASIS.

1976 through 2016

ref. US Census Bureau, Economics Indicator Division. 2/7/17

The cumulative negative balance of trade since 1975 came in at the astonishing number of $14.2 trillion. Offset by roughly $ 3.2 trillion of income from the services sector, that is a negative number of $11.2 trillion, still an incredible number which written out is 11,200,000,000,000 dollars. Casting an eye at our Nation's debt clock showed our debt stood at an even bigger number, but was not surprised for I knew the Government had not been balancing the Federal budget and assumed that made up for the difference. Being a cash and carry business, that trade deficits would have been covered by cash and so borrowing was what one would have suspected. Thus, the number I now needed to check was what had that cumulative number been over the same period of time?

Ever the one that liked to dot the I's and cross the T's, I wanted to close the loop on what if any had been the role of our Leaders and politicians in this story and so turned my attention to that Budget. Wait, was there anything else I needed to look at before leaving that subject. Of course, the Department of Commerce had noted in several places that the numbers from the trade of illegal drugs were not included and they had in fact made some estimates of what those amounts might have been and had in fact incorporated the thinking of other Government Agencies in those yearly estimates, while also noting the imports of heroin had recently been declining as our domestic production of synthetics had been increasing. Adding those numbers up and translating to an annual drug trade of $125 billion a year, it added up over forty-two years to the staggering amount of $5.2 trillion, which being cash flowing out of our Country had to be included. Some other miscellaneous deductions were added to cover unreported amounts spent on wars and monies still to be removed from our Country added another $2.2 trillion to the deficit with the final number as follows:

1976-2016 CUMULATIVE TRADE DEFICIT
(US $ trillion)

Goods Exports Less Imports*	-14.2
Services Exports Less Imports	3.2
Illegal Drug Imports**	-5.2
Foreign Wars, etc.***	-2.2
TOTAL	-18.4

*When measuring job gains or losses, the goods number is what is used as it reflects manufacturing rather than services, which covers; transportation, travel, insurance, royalties, and other non-manufacturing transactions.

** USCB estimate, equivalent to an average of $125 billion per year.

*** I regard this as a debatable number. The impact of foreign wars on our balance of payments has varied from minus $3 trillion to as high as $7 trillion depending on the assumptions and what is included, and further has in some cases been accounted for elsewhere. The whole subject of balance of payments is fraught with problems such as what is happening to the profits foreign owned shipping and manufacturing companies have on deposit here in the USA and yet is potentially going to be repatriated back overseas? Conversely, estimates on the amount of profits being held by USA companies overseas that can be repatriated to the USA are estimated to be close to $2.5 trillion. Perhaps all this in turn is overshadowed by the $6.6 trillion (as of year-end 2016) of Treasury Bonds being held by overseas countries. Suffice to say a variance of less than plus or minus 10% does not change this message.

$$$$$

THE USA BUDGET

With our decision to allocate trade cash flow losses to accumulative debt, and in all honesty solely because these purchases have to be made in cash and debt is the only convenient and instantaneous way in which they can be paid (Bank Drafts), we need to test that decision against the next category of spending, the Nation's Budget.

There was no surprise here in that the cumulative numbers were again hidden, this time if possible even more so than our trade data, but then we are dealing with politicians. Despite them, we added up the yearly data for 42 years arriving at the obscene number of $13.4 trillion. Realizing we would have to search for how much money our treasury Department had printed to cover those shortfalls, for the money had to come from somewhere else due to already having allocated 100% of our debt to cover trade losses. While not exact, my best estimate of 2% per year based on our Nation's GNP was $8.2 trillion, a number I was not surprised at for inflation though meant to be gradual and needed for growth had in fact been pretty awful, especially when one considers our politicians had been manipulating the cost of living index to keep Social Security payments low displacing needed things like food with TV costs! Still facing a gap of $5.2 trillion, a huge number in itself, I went digging into the Government records.

After three months of research, what unfolded was a story so deeply hidden that no adjectives can describe what was discovered, and then only by digging into the records of the Treasury Department and the Federal Reserve Bank, for we already knew they were staffed by honorable people, that even if pressured by the dishonest, would defy them. And so, we come to one of the worst tales of deceit and dishonesty that has ever been perpetrated on the American People.

During the Great Depression, when our leaders and politicians were struggling over the problem of trying to cover the outflow of cash from our country (to cover the cost of buying imports), they started to cast their eyes on the money lying idle and gathering interest in the Social Security Trust Fund. (At that time the Treasury Department, as they received our payroll deposits, would issue Treasury Notes that were marketable and interest bearing. That meant that the people managing the Trust Fund could instantly convert those notes back into cash and issue retirement checks to their Social Security Retirees). After all, this was the people's money that had been deducted from paychecks and taxation to cover their future retirement and pension payments, and was rightfully theirs.

Moving into the 1970's and ignoring this fact, efforts continued to try and find a way to transfer that money out of that Trust and into the Government's General Account where it could then be used for any purpose our politicians and leaders wanted. Finally deciding that outright confiscation combined with secrecy was the only possible way, they proceeded to instruct the Treasury Dept. to siphon off the money from the Social Security Trust fund into the General Ledger account. And this is where the so-called brilliance of these schemers showed itself in of all places the FEDS Notes of 8th Oct. 2015. In the end, the Treasury was instructed to issue Treasury Bonds to that so-called 'Trust Fund' that were non-marketable (could not be sold or transferred to anyone else), were non-interest bearing (changing the current interest-bearing bonds instantaneously to zero yields), and were 'not in the concept of federal debt' (the Federal Government would not recognize the bonds as being debt and therefore not being repayable). In other words, in essence, the Social Security payroll deductions both past and future were to be considered as general revenue tax payments and not contributions to the Social Security Trust Fund with neither interest nor repayment necessary. (This meant that the Social Security Trustees could no longer convert deposits into cash for the treasury notes were non-marketable. Indeed, if in fact the Treasury Department wanted to return some of that money, they would first have to go to our politicians and ask for the Nation's Debt ceiling to be raised first, and only then face the problem of being able to pay out money to an account that was now labelled as 'not being payable in the concept of Federal Debt!)

A catch twenty-two comes next, for the short term monthly deposits are still issued regular interest-bearing notes and are moved back and forth into cash to meet monthly variations. Thus, some politician can jump up and say rubbish, Social Security is still being given marketable and interest-bearing bonds and so would be correct, but so typical of a lawyer's response for 99% of politicians are lawyers! Never-the-less that answer is a distortion of the truth and evidently, when President Obama asked this same question, that was the answer he was given.

Unknown is whether or not he ever learned the real story. Over the subsequent years, this practice was continued and expanded to include the Pension Trust Funds of our Military and Civil Servants, and with them too being drained until nothing was left. If ever there was outright theft, this was it. And this was the public's pension money that had been stolen, including from our veterans. So much for all the bombast and claims by our leaders and politicians of looking after those who have served. The perfidy then got worse, if that were possible. There was one Pension Trust Fund left still intact. Can anyone guess which one it was? Why nothing less than the one that pays out the pensions to our Leaders and Politicians! And this my fellow Americans is what is going on in our Country. And now to the last chapter in this story of deceit and corruption. Our Nation's Debt Clock is not run by our Government, and they refused to accept this theft from our Trust and Pension Funds as being non-repayable and added that $5 trillion back into the debt number! (For the curious who want to check the truth of the above, they would need to penetrate the many layers of reports and data to find it, so, to save time and effort please see the section in 'End Notes" at the end of this book for copies of the pertinent data.

The numbers speak for themselves. Our Politicians have been spending more and more money in the form of welfare payments to keep their voters happy while not increasing taxes on the wealthy to pay for these programs.

1976-2016 CUMULATIVE BUDGET DEFICIT
(Trillion US$)

Cumulative Budget Deficit since 1976	-13.4
Paid for by printing currency	8.2
Paid for by removing money from Trust Funds	5.3

Likewise, trade has been linked to the accumulation of wealth by those with positive trade balances. On the other hand, if negative, those poor people are heading for nothing but trouble. And so, what are the numbers on the USA telling us? We are the ones heading for nothing but trouble!

Let's start by looking at what the inflation target has been for the Treasury Department. While it has varied over the forty-two years being looked at, 2% of GNP is not a bad number to use. Compounded, over forty-two years with a starting GNP of $6 trillion, that escalation results in an ending GNP of $14 trillion, with the actual being slightly over $17 trillion. However, with the Federal Reserve Bank's recognized debt being $14 trillion that tells us something. The other relevant numbers are:

-The printed money total, to meet inflation targets, is $8 trillion ($14 - 6 = 8).

-The National Debt Grew by $14 trillion ($19.5 less a starting number of $0.5 and less $5 from Trust Funds = $14 trillion.)

We realize this is a hard concept to understand, but if we were to imagine us being a shop in a mall, and spending more money each year than we made, how would one cover those dollars flowing out from our cash register? Now, try to imagine we had a printer that could print dollar bills. We could have a choice, either print that money or borrow it. Now imagine what would happen if people found out we were printing it in the back room. One of two things would happen; our money would have less value or people would not accept our currency. Neither choice would work in the long run with either closing our store or declaring bankruptcy the options. At that point, borrowing is the only option, and in this example, we simply print the dollars we borrow, for the lender is ourselves! And this is the practice that has been perpetrated on us by our leaders and politicians. And now comes the killer situation: those same people have begun to realize that with the publicly known amount of our accumulated debt now reaching $20 trillion, sooner or later our dollars will become worthless and others will then no longer accept our currency as payment. While the exact amount when this will happen is unknown, all know it can't be far away. Even worse is yet to come, for those same people think it is because we can't seem to be able to balance our National Budget. That is not the issue but is being caused by losing money on trade.! All this has been shown to be the problem throughout history, and without money, everyone loses wealth. And without that wealth, we cannot afford to buy things, and without that power very quickly lose leadership, for who wants to have someone as a leader who can't even manage their finances? What comes next is both shameful and humbling.

Without cash, or having to display to the world the need to borrow it or do without, everybody begins to understand just how weak and powerless one becomes. Worse, they can see people unemployed that have to rely on welfare to make ends meet. In turn, one's National and State Budgets also become more difficult to balance.

$$$$$

Are Trade and Budget numbers inextricably linked together? No, for the management of one's domestic Budget is a separate and distinct management issue. Only a Trade gain or loss affects cash flow and the management of it by Debt. The question is where do we go from here?

Between the Federal Reserve Bank and our Treasury Department, they have done a magnificent job in keeping our Country out of trouble, but at the same time, they are only too well aware of their limitations. Nobody knows the exact number when debt reaches the psychological point of 'being too much'. Suffice to say, lenders are already showing signs of nervousness with some saying publicly they will no longer purchase Treasury notes, or in the case of foreign countries, no longer accept US dollars in payment for goods. The killer though, was when the consortium of World Leaders stated they were planning to reduce the role of the US dollar as a back-up currency. When interest rates are artificially depressed, as they have been in the USA, (to hold down what should have been massive costs in our Nation's Budget and the normal way to discourage people from over-borrowing). There are eventually consequences, one of which I posit is for others to reduce their perceived risk to that currency. With the USA already setting limits to the printing of money (2% of GDP growth), that avenue is also closed leaving the further issuing of debt the only option. Debasement, or the printing of money, is something resorted to when debt is not an option and has been a step demonstrated through thousands of years of history to lead to inflation, financial collapse, and bankruptcy. With a dysfunctional Congress, what are the chances they can not only figure out the solution but to unify and pass the necessary legislation to make that happen? Indeed, can one imagine the only other solution being a change to the Government's way of book-keeping? Rather than speculate on such an uncertain subject, let's move on to the real solution.

$$$$$

THE USA'S DOMESTIC INDUSTRIAL PRODUCTION

Why, starting in 1975, did our manufacturing base close?

1.) In the 1960's and 1970's, we began to see imported items being offered at some very low prices. Quality was usually awful preventing a mass exodus to those products. However, by the late 1960's, efforts by such people as Deming in Japan, were starting to make exports from there, of better quality than those made here in the USA. While marginally cheaper than our own, Japanese cars for example, were becoming of better quality and variety, and as a result caught our own industry off guard.

2.) During this same period, we were becoming more aware of pollution as a health and environmental factor. Recognizing that cleanup steps had to be taken, our Government passed legislation mandating that corrective action be enacted. However, in order to avoid making enemies of industry, and their many political donors, Congress passed some very unusual legislation. Establishing the 'Environmental Protection Agency', as the Government body to take on the responsibility of cleaning up our Country, they also delegated to it that they set their own targets and regulations to achieve that objective. (Hopefully to divert anger away from the Congress onto that Agency?) No matter, over the ensuing years, many industries found it was economically unfeasible to comply with these new Laws, deciding to shut down and invest or even worse, just purchase what they needed from overseas countries. These decisions were based on two factors:

-Their own costs from a combination of having to either modernize existing facilities or having to build new ones. (With no Government incentives such as fast write-offs, subsidies, or financing assistance). In this calculation, no consideration was given to the fallout of these closures on local communities, lost jobs, the impact on Government Budgets, both Local, State, and Federal. Least of all, to the downstream industries reliant on them for business. Last, and seemingly of no concern was the effect it would have on our National Security, and worst of all, to our Balance of Trade position! There was another key decision-making factor, the time needed to gain approval for these new plants, for if lengthy, it could well dictate what would happen.

- Their cost of building these new plants in other countries either by themselves or with third parties. These decisions were guided by the lack of environmental regulations there, the financial assistance they could get, both capital and write-offs, the location and cost of the nearest raw materials, and of course the local cost of labor. Interestingly enough, while some revue procedures within our Federal Bureaucracies were set up, none impacted on either past decision making, or on how future regulations should be promulgated. Missing was a public review and critique of that process.

3.)   The consequences of the above were: Within ten years, the entire Steel Industry was gone, with only recycling and a few specialty plants remaining. (With S. Korea and China, the beneficiaries who gave their respective Industries the money and incentives to build these new plants.) We are not done yet, for the worst was yet to come. The shipbuilding industry, with their main source of raw material gone (steel), now proceeded to leave the USA (with S. Korea and China again the beneficiaries). Not even worth mentioning were all the other smaller supply businesses that left as a result of those closures.

-It is only fitting that we end with an issue affecting Trade, Oil, Shipping, and the EPA/IMO. Long overdue is an effort to reduce our shipping industry's pollution levels with marine engine emission still at 1965 standards. Likewise, the fuel they use is typically high sulfur at 2%-3.5 % sulfur content. Effective in July of 2015, EPA, with IMO (United Nations Marine section's approval), set fuel standards for all ships in USA coastal waters at 0.1% Sulfur content levels. Also, these levels were extended to cover all USA marine use worldwide. Meanwhile until perhaps as late as 2025, the rest of the world's marine traffic are free to continue to use of up to 3.5% sulfur bunker fuel (or less in European and Scandinavian coastal waters). Meanwhile, with multiple tanks for fuel, (switchable at the press of a button) only one or two need to be dedicated for low sulfur fuel use in those restricted waters, with the rest holding high Sulfur bunker oil for international water travel. In practical terms, with a 50% higher cost for low-sulfur fuel, this puts any USA merchant vessel out of business. However, there is good news. There are none left! (Of the 175 left as of the end of 2016, 152 are suitable for military use and the balance for intra-USA traffic). If the understanding of the story above is correct, then we submit that much of our problem on trade is of our own making. In addition, an extensive overhaul of the decision making in the EPA and Congress is long overdue. A friend of mine in the Oil Tanker business smirked when he read this. Fred, he said, don't you know these foreign flag Captains don't press that low expensive low sulfur fuel button until an inspector is around? Believe me, they are not going to do so unless fines are threatened.

4.) At the other end of this story is what has happened to our High Technology industry. Here we include our Communications, TV, Telephone, Computer, Medical, and Electronic Industries. With much of the research and development being done in this Country, how is it that today virtually everything is manufactured overseas, and even if not, then the parts are, with our role being solely to be an assembler in this Country? Clearly something is far wrong, but what? First there is no enforcement of USA patent protection and so foreign producers can make those products with impunity. Second come incentives! Let us take a look at the top ten exporters to the USA; China, Japan, Taiwan, S. Korea and a whole host of European Countries. With investment capital or incentive being provided from their Central Governments, and the construction of whole new Cities, factory buildings, and training being thrown in without charge, and export incentives added when needed, who wouldn't build plants there. In Germany, a one or two-year write-off is almost standard with smiles from Guilds and Unions the envy of others on the outside. Then throw in renewable energy, training, and other incentives and you get the idea. Meanwhile back in the USA regulations, approval delays and no breaks are the rule. As for manufacturing secrets, Patents and other skills, those are being stolen with hardly a whimper from our politicians for some of their biggest donors are the same importers of those products. There is only one snag, the companies that have chosen to invest overseas are faced with Taxes, not only in those countries, but also in the USA whenever those profits are brought back. Estimated to be well over $2.5 trillion at the end of 2016, the question is; should we give them a break?

We need to learn from how China, Germany, and S. Korea are attracting industries and jobs. However, we also need to correct our mistakes. And both of these steps can be done without threatening anyone with higher Import Duties. For there is yet another factor, we need to address. First, one has to be crazy to have allowed whole industries to shut down or disappear that are essential to our Nation's survival and security. If that was not bad enough, most of those industries are supported by our taxpayers and should be forced to purchase from USA companies here in the USA. With virtually every other nation protecting these industries and end uses, I doubt anyone would challenge us from making these moves. In fact, they may be laughing their heads off as to why it has taken us so long to make this correction. (For those that live in the D.C. area, next time you go to Dulles Airport, look at the major work going on extending the rail line to the airport. You will see nothing but foreign excavating equipment. It should all be American with jobs for Americans, and what's wrong with that!) A partial listing of items that should be mandated to be done by ourselves is:

> Infrastructure and Government supplies.
> Military equipment and materials.
> High Tech Essentials.
> Medical/Hospital/Pharmaceutical.
> Finance/Insurance.
> Transport. (Including shipping to and from the USA.)
> Energy.
> Basic Foods.

(The above covers all levels of Government, both local and Federal. Also disallowed would be imports of parts and would require raw materials, if unavailable locally, to be stockpiled). In 2016, of our total imports of goods, ($2.3 trillion.) the above listing accounted for some $1.3 trillion of that total. In other words, if enacted our trade deficit would have been changed from a $0.7 deficit into a $0.6 positive balance.

Trusting that the above makes sense to everyone, a second step would be the adoption of incentives to speed up the process. If we look at the top two World Trading Countries, what else do we find? They provide and dictate investments for their industry, either by direct Government funding or by giving private investors one or two-year write-off incentives for new facilities and improvements. In America, rarely given by Government and certainly not for anything over a million dollars, and then often disallowed by State Governments. (Easy to neutralize, by providing for offsetting adjustments to any State distributions of Federal payments.) We need to make sure our industries find it attractive to invest here and to remove any and all obstacles put in their way.

Thirdly, remaining imports should meet our own environmental, employment, health, and currency standards else we would have done nothing to help the World's problems. Rarely does cheap labor alone dictate where goods are made, but rather it has been decided for a host of reasons, and those should be considered when making changes to import or export economics.

Third, we should add another word to the phrase 'Free Trade.' 'Fair and Free Trade.' The reality is that nearly all countries restrict imports to only those they cannot make themselves.

A caution is needed here. Legislation on the above needs to spell out that on all bids and expenditures, labor, equipment, and supplies need to be sourced from American owned and operated companies located in the USA. Also, any State or Local Authority that chooses not to comply with that requirement shall lose eligibility to that and all future Federally Funded Projects.

$$\$\$\$\$\$$

MANUFACTURING AND JOBS

The next question we asked was, are the job targets President Trump set achievable? With the USA keeping track of imports by business and job center, and in turn publishing the data on our Gross Domestic Product by these same categories, we can calculate the impact that imports have on jobs, and in turn, the expected job impact of reversing these trends. Assuming we adopted the changes, we have suggested on what should be manufactured here in the USA; this can give us the answer. One would then add the expected multiplier effect. However, we did not do so to factor in the effect of many of these jobs being incremental, and also being in new facilities and the most advanced in labor efficiency. The above plus small business growth indicates that the fifteen-million target seems to be realistic.

While not calculated, if taxable, for the above number is GDP growth, that kind of income growth would solve our Budget Deficit and Debt problems overnight. Once and for all proving that a positive Trade Balance, which the above would give us, solves the other two.

The temptation when looking at trade statistics is to overlook the complications that arise if one adopts draconian actions on any individual section of our economy without considering the future growth and trends in that industry with transportation being a prime example.

When we consider the implications of self-driving cars, the computer optimization of shared driving for commuters and freight deliverers, and the inevitable move to electrically driven vehicles to reduce carbon dioxide levels, we can start to appreciate the incredible changes that are coming. (See our book on climate change in this series). High-speed road travel, less congestion on our roads and in our cities, will be only one factor. With computer control will also come standardization, the linking up to form high-speed trains of vehicles making highway speed even faster with slipstreaming and better fuel efficiency diverting air travel to highway for journeys of less than 750 miles.

2017-2021 JOB POTENTIAL CALCULATION
(All data in $ billions and jobs in thousands)

	GDP	FACTOR	JOBS
Durable Manufacturing	650	0.38	247
Non-Durable Manufacturing	2,180	5.45	11,881
Construction	140	10.90	1,526
Mining	100	3.00	300
Corp. Management	100	6.40	640
Oil & Gas	100	3.00	300
Solar etc.	400	6.00	2.400
Agriculture	65	12.20	793
TOTAL	3,735	4.84	18,087

These changes provide the opportunities for converting these industries to be essential and served by American-owned and manufacturing companies is obvious. Let the automobile companies make their cars and pick-ups where they want for they can see no further than their noses. The cars of the future will be far different with less personalization, standard for highway speed-trains, all electric with little need for fuel oils, almost no insurance, and in the cities half the traffic, quiet, and no auto pollution. It will be a different World with all but long-distance air-travel a thing of the past. Gone will be the need for City airports with rural locations the future. Try to imagine New York with fifty percent of all vehicle and seventy-five percent of all truck traffic gone, virtually all parking a thing of the past, no more fossil fuel vehicles and smelly exhausts, no need for car or cab horns, and to complete the story, silent electric vehicles and only rarely the sound of airplanes overhead. One can only try and imagine the impact it will have on people's decisions on where they want to live.

If the UK and the USA tackled the same issues, namely machinery, vehicles, and oil, the problem would be half solved.

If we then added in the products and construction that should be done and managed by each of them, a positive balance of payments would result allowing both to pay-off their long-term debts.

2016 USA TRADE PRODUCT BALANCES
(USDC $ Billion)

	Imports	Exports	Balance
Total	2252	1454	-798
Electrical Machinery	336	167	-169
Machinery, Computers	315	191	-124
Vehicles	285	124	-161
Fuels, Oil	163	95	-68
Pharmaceuticals	93	47	-46
Optical, Tech, Medical	81	82	1
Gems, Gold, etc.	67	57	-10
Furniture, etc.	63	5	-58
Plastics	50	58	8
Organic Chemicals	50	34	-16
Aircraft	31	135	104

$$$$$

CAN OUR GOLD RESERVES SAVE US?

Unfortunately our gold reserves would not even cover one year's trade deficit. In fact with them being used to cover market shorting of gold, (To keep its market value low) even Germany was not allowed to inspect its gold reportedly held in the Fort Knox depository and who in fact it belonged to. More openly is the Bank of England's depository which is shown below. In any event the US Treasury Report of 9/30/18 shows total holdings of gold at 261million fine troy ounces which at a current market value of $1,215 per ounce equals $317 billion. Hardly an impressive figure compared to our latest estimated 2018 trade deficit of S600 billion.

BANK OF ENGLAND GOLD DEPOSITORY

$$$$$

CHAPTER VI

MODERNIZING OUR INFRASTRUCTURE

(CONVERTING ELECTRICITY PRODUCTION FROM FOSSIL TO RENEWABLE ENERGY FUELS.)

I feel a little bit like a phony on this subject, for truth be told, the Electrical Producing Utilities, Transmission, and Electrical Storage Companies have been doing an outstanding job for our Country. Aided by the various State and Government Agencies, The DOE, EIA, and a host of business and research organizations, generating plants, transmission lines, energy storage and batteries are being constantly updated and being replaced with the most advanced technology available on an annual basis. Included in this work has been a mix of tried and true methods coupled with the testing of many new technologies such that when proven they can be introduced without risk into our system. And, just to cap it all off, doing all this with self-financing. All in all, almost the perfect balance to optimize efficiency at the lowest possible cost. Indeed, my only concern is whether or not our Government can give this industry the right goals and incentives to follow for the future. The details in my Chapter on this subject parrot industry wisdom, but hopefully is written in understandable English for non-electrical people.

There was only one part of this subject that should be mentioned, for it involves our political relations with Canada. Already one of the World's leaders in the production of Hydroelectric power, Canada is bringing on stream another 6 GW capacity in the next three years. However, they have the potential to add another 75 GW on top of that. If we can work with Canada to add as much of that to supplement our own needs here in the USA, that would make our job that much easier. In turn, that added export business might be most welcome as it would offset the implied reduction of fossil fuel sales to the USA.

$$$$$

CONVERTING THE TRANSPORTATION SYSTEM FROM FOSSIL TO RENEWABLE ELECTRIC ENERGY FUELS.

This part of our research was the most complicated for it involves road, rail and air travel, and how much of it would have to remain on fossil sources of energy, given today's technology. After that came the assessment of how renewable energy would be supplied and to where. Factoring into all this was the question of whether or not we should encourage the construction of a high-speed rail system such as we find in China and Europe, all to replace much of our inter-city air travel. With the advent of automated driving of cars and trucks, and the talk in turn of that changing the industry from the ownership of vehicles to a 'ride-hailing' system for commuting and recreational driving, led to the need to develop some projections that ended up eliminating growth from the equation, i.e. a flat demand case.

The biggest challenge was how these steps could be financed, given the fact that our Nation already has Debts totaling $20 trillion and Trade deficits running at $0.7 trillion per year, making the option of Government financing almost a non-starter. With incomes still flat, suddenly adding taxes or fossil fuel energy penalties, to pay for these changes, would be difficult. So, what was the practical solution? To put in place a series of gradual tax penalties and incentives that would give buyers and sellers adequate warning of what was coming such that efficiencies and savings to consumers would offset each other. For example, in the case of automobiles and trucks, imposing a gradual yearly tax on gasoline and diesel fuels, with an incentive to use electric or hybrid vehicles, would alert auto companies to downsize vehicles and improve mileage to offset those costs. Similarly, buyers would also be alerted to make purchase or lease decisions that they could afford. Unfortunately, that calculation has to factor in a reducing fossil fuel use each year. Settling on an escalating tax of 20 cents per year, after 16 years it will have raised $5 trillion, and over twenty $7 trillion. The good news is that if all of that effort and investment is sourced in the USA rather than imported, then the Nation's GNP will increase resulting in increases in tax collections and Government budget surpluses. (Assuming our politicians don't mess that up.)

What does that search show?

1) When moving the USA to renewable energy, especially as we near 100%, the problem becomes one of matching an erratic 24-hour source of supply to an erratic 24-hour demand with a 50% swing in any 24-hour period. It is all about balancing that system which is contained in that chapter with corrective measures for both sides of the equation. Regardless, the problem of storing energy remains. With several options, some of which have yet to be commercially proven, the regrettable fact is that the only immediate way of solving that issue is for the USA to retain a large capacity of natural gas fired plants on a stand-by basis, and ready to fill those gaps. As an example, for huge cities that may demand large amounts of electricity for air conditioning on hot days, that can swing peak power supply loads upwards by 10-15%. Something that is yet to be proven and supplied by renewable sources. We also have to remember that these plants need to be located

as near as possible to where the needs are and that these vary with the region served. The good news is that these newer natural gas units are highly efficient and emit the lowest amounts of CO_2 of any plant in existence. Add to that being run only to fill short term peaks, and you have the ideal and most economical solution.

2) Hydroelectric is already under threat of losing its main source of summer water from glaciers, making this a questionable source for the future. The challenge ahead may be the ability to store monsoon rains, though not many areas have that capability with Ethiopia the exception. An ideal option, for those units, while having some seasonal variations in supply, is to be able to store energy in the form of pumped water to higher elevations and ready to increase power output from the generators below.

3) Nuclear, if sited carefully can be an option, but it too has the continuing difficulty of requiring large amounts of cooling water, something that is of increasing concern. Longer term, Thorium and a hot salt circulation system might hold promise with as yet the first plant still to be built using this technology.

4) Coal has yet to show any signs of becoming a zero emissions fuel, and here we don't include the idea of pumping CO_2 emissions into an underground cavern as being an acceptable answer. A far better idea would be to insist that the many new plants required to build renewable energy equipment, be built in coal mining areas. And here, we include replacement transportation for rail, air, and highway movement.

5) For those that can economically install solar rooftop energy systems, that is the most efficient way of solving the problem. Those rooftop systems usually omit the best system of all, a roof water heating system that can replace interior, electric and gas water units. (Typically account for 10-20% of heating bills.). For new or remodeled homes, another option to be considered should be switching to a rooftop hot water heating system for the house. While needing stand-by electricity to meet demand during low sun periods, given the right rooftop direction and unshaded units, it can be an economically sound and environmentally friendly alternative. Without question, solar farms are the wave of the future as energy storage becomes an option.

6) The Wind is rarely a practicable way to generate power for homeowners but is a practical method of generation for large scale users and utility companies.

7) Other methods of generating power are geothermal, tidal, biomass, etc. All of which are more for special situations.

8) The best was saved to last. For those driving electric or hybrid cars, were you aware that the economics of rooftop solar are improved if for that use? The reason is that gasoline and diesel are higher cost fuels compared to the cost of household electricity. Thus, as the USA swings to more electrically driven cars, so the economics of rooftop solar will improve. All we need is an incentive. If implemented as a tax on gasoline, diesel, and kerosene fuels, and rebated for solar (or per capita utility wind and solar farm investments), these are the amounts of money that would be available to subsidize these investments;

$1/gallon, $2.5 trillion over 16 years (declining balance).
$2/gallon, $5.1 trillion over 16 years (declining balance).
$3/gallon, $7.6 trillion over 16 years (declining balance).

All one would have to do on this 'no-brainer,' is to ask anyone in the renewable energy business what this would mean for our Nation.

Make no mistake; the technology race is on for electricity storage at several levels. Both encouraging and yet frustrating is the way so many options and uses by others have been blocked by patents, all held in the hope they can generate money for the holders, but at the same time block that idea from general usage. Perhaps a signal that a 'Manhattan Type Project' has come again, with progress and gains to be shared by all? What is happening today is both a slow and expensive way of finding an answer, neither of which we have in plenty. As an example, the most efficient and lowest cost battery storage systems are in the range of $150 kWh for utility companies and $300 kWh for home storage units.

$$$$$

MODERNIZING TRANSPORTATION

Our timing might just be superb for we are not only entering into an age with little use of fossil fuels, but also into one of automation and innovation such that our Country's entire infrastructure needs to be modernized.

If planned and handled correctly, coordinated with our Trading Policy, and paid for by modernizing our Governments accounting methods, this change could completely change America, our balance of payments, our debt structure, and lead us into a golden age of job training, wealth distribution never mind less road and air traffic, less noise, less pollution, and greater security and independence, but more importantly more space in our cities and a better lifestyle. Let me explain.

Oil is the supplier to our transportation industries. What is coming is no less than a complete revolution involving computerization, the development of advanced automated driving, ride sharing, freight sharing software with emphasis on reducing commuter and freight traffic on our main highways and in our cities. Simultaneous will be the move from combustion engines to electrical based on renewable energy. Just think what this will mean:

A). First will come cars and trucks able to drive themselves.

B). These will be quickly followed by programs allowing ride-sharing, freight sharing complete with automated loading and unloading of goods.

C). Next will come third-party ownership of rides on an as needed basis, again shared.

D). Last will come train formation where trucks, buses and autos are formed into connected units able to travel on dedicated train only roads. These will be up to 50% more energy efficient and be travelling at 35% higher speeds, all from streamlining efficiency gains. This means road traffic will be moving at an average speed of 150 miles per hour.

All four of the above steps will be taking place at the same time as road transportation moves from oil use to electric.

All four of the above steps will be occurring as ownership and the need for insurance is phased out.

All four of these steps will be occurring as oil production, oil tankers, oil refineries and gas stations disappear.

All four of these steps will be occurring while Cities become quieter, pollution free, have 65% less traffic, are replacing parking and gas station areas with parks, and higher density apartment living.

All four of these steps will be occurring as short haul air traffic (750 mile or less trips) switch from air to high-speed road trains.

Inevitably, as vehicles move from individual to fleet ownership, so they will they become more standardized and therefore of lower cost to produce.

With the mandate that the above has to be built and manufactured by USA owned and operated companies here in the USA, the scope and size of the above implies a vast re-investment in the USA with even automation required to reduce the incredible growth pressures on added labor needs.

AND THIS IS WHAT THE BUILDING OF A NEW AND MODERN INFRASTRUCTURE IN AMERICA IS ALL ABOUT, SOMETHING THAT EVEN A DYSFUNCTIONAL CONGRESS MAY BE ABLE TO PASS! AND WE ARE NOT DONE YET!

$$$$$

OCEAN TRANSPORT

One of the greatest opportunities for the USA to recover one of its lost basic businesses is ocean transport. While this is part of trade services rather than goods, because our Maritime fleet is virtually zero[4] anything we do would be an improvement and have a positive effect on our trade balance. The other reason is that the condition of the World's current fleet is a disgrace and needs to be modernized immediately.

Having said that, history tells us that one must also control ones shipping business in order to be a successful trader for safety, efficiency, speed, and reliability are everything. Thus having double hulled vessels for transporting oil and other hazardous materials is both a national security issue, but more importantly, a must for environmental safety reasons.

From an environmental point of view the EPA's requirement that US ships be required to run on fuel oil of 0.1% or less sulfur content is a step in the right direction. However with the USA having virtually no fleet left, it will only penalize our tiny shipping industry for the rest of the World is operating on bunker fuel which is typically oil of 3% sulfur content and half the price.[5]

So, what should we do? We should mandate that only USA owned and operated vessels be allowed to carry our imports and exports with a timetable this be met by 2050 with that date far out for the following reasons:

Hopefully if such a program is started promptly, it would mean the USA would have to build up to 4,000 large vessels which would require a vast ship

---

[4] We still have military use vessels on hand plus a handful left for USA to USA shipments which are mandated to be USA owned and operated, otherwise it is no more along with the steel industry.
[5] The UN has also mandated a change to 1% or less fuel oil by 2030 with that date in jeopardy as ship registration just moves to non UN nations which do not have to comply with that order.

construction industry be created with even 2050 perhaps not enough time to complete such a task, never mind the vast support industries that would be involved.

From an environmental point of view the World's current fleet is a disgrace with ships undermanned and poorly trained, especially at the senior level with often only a mate on board whereas safety demands a captain and first and second mates be aboard. Oil and other hazardous products are usually shipped in single hulled vessels with that compounded by having over-large tanks such that any hull breech results in massive spills. Additionally, ship engines are usually outdated as far as fuel efficiency is concerned resulting in air pollution far in excess of what it should be. As an example, any modern fleet should have the latest design of marine engine which for those not familiar with those developments would be LNG[6] based with pollution levels almost zero, and in the event of a sinking, the sturdier tanks required to hold it would be less likely to fracture. However, if by chance it did release, evaporating into the air would eliminate the current disastrous oil slick damage that typically ensues..

Obvious should be the fact that ships be registered, fully manned with properly qualified and trained crews, have at their disposal all modern navigation, location, and communication equipment. Despite automation and reduced manning needs, all ships should be properly protected against pirate attack with communication with other ships and our military automatically alerted.

Another thing that should be incorporated is the improved propeller design along with a caging system to eliminate the horrendous damage being done to the Ocean's large sea-life. And while we are at it, proper on board sewage system tanks should be mandatory with recycling systems preferred. All-in-all there is no reason the USA should not have the safest, cleanest, and environmentally friendly ships in the World, which should immediately be mandated by our Government.

$$$$$

AIR TRANSPORT

Air fails for three reasons. No replacement has been found as yet for fossil fuel. Second, air is noisy, expensive, and, when we add in travel to and from airports, a crumbling airport infrastructure, and security issues, a relatively expensive and time-consuming way of travel. The nail in the coffin for that industry is the fact that all near term dreams of cheap and low-cost pollution free

---

[6] Liquid Natural Gas.

air travel hinge on the discovery of ultra-light electric battery technology, something yet to be discovered.

The decision by most travelers to fly or drive to their destination is based on travel time and convenience. If one had to make a trip of four hundred miles and had two choices of how to get there, with the first being one's automatically driven car taking three hours door to door from your home to your destination. The second is of course by air involving driving to your local airport, buying a ticket, checking in, perhaps involving checking baggage, waiting for the plane's departure time, hopefully not delayed, then loading, and finally the flight with seemingly ever decreasing service. Once at the other end, the whole process reverses with waiting for baggage the usual nightmare. Then comes the cab ride or car rental to your final destination. Total time six hours, if you are lucky. Who on earth would make that choice? In fact, today, 95% of people choose to drive for a four-hundred-miles or less journey with only 3% by air[7].

Let's take a look at a 750-mile journey. That travel time for automated vehicles increases from three to six hours, whereas the air travel time only increases from six to seven-hours. Today, that same study indicates that 35% of travelers chose air before, whereas with these revised times it would change to only 3%. Thus, as high-speed road becomes more efficient, so too will air traffic decline.

The why is simple; time and convenience. The high-speed road will be the game changer for our world. If we doubt that, just think, a seven-hundred-and-fifty-mile radius from any major USA, European or Asian City would cover vast travel centers resulting in a switch of 75% of all air traffic to road. Some examples of what a 750-mile radius covers are:

Washington, DC: Quebec City, Toronto, Chicago, Nashville, Atlanta, Jacksonville.
San Francisco: Seattle, Salt Lake City, Phoenix, San Diego.
London: all the UK, via the tunnel, all of Europe.
Paris: All of Europe.
Rome: All of mainland Europe except Spain.
Berlin: All of Europe except Madrid.
Istanbul: All of Eastern Europe, West Russia, and the Middle East.
Shanghai: All of China.
Delhi: Karachi, Mumbai, Hyderabad, Calcutta.

---

[7] USDC Study.

We could expand the list, but the impact on air travel around the world would be extraordinary. The nail in the coffin for the airline industry is the fact that all near term dreams of cheap and low-cost pollution free air travel hinge on the discovery of ultra-light electric battery technology, something that has yet to be discovered. Obviously, we need to retain the long-range portion of that industry along with carbon fuels, but with stricter emission standards, which incidentally are being ignored as of this writing.

One last thought about renewable energy: while the cost of fuel is zero, depreciation and interest costs will offset some of those reductions, but on an incremental basis, and on a balance of trade basis, the impact would be amazing, not to mention the zero emission levels.

WE SHOULD CHANGE TO RENEWABLE ENERGY REGARDLESS OF POPULATION GROWTH AND CLIMATE CHANGE.

$$$$$

MILITARY

Over the centuries, money and technology has driven that industry every bit as much, if not more than military generalship. In our modern times that has only increased the quandary of keeping something secret versus its use and inevitable disclosure. The other question has been how to hide how it is manufactured. I would submit that all military supplies, including parts, should be manufactured here by USA owned and operated Companies, with security and secrecy being the justification. With much of it already being done, tightening that requirement even further to include parts should not pose a problem.

$$$$$

AGRICULTURE

In the event of worldwide supply problems, it would seem to make common sense that most of our food supplies should be coming from domestic sources that we can control. The only question is really what percent that should be, for when shortages hit, that point is too late to do anything about it except rationing. For staples, it should be 100% and luxury items something less and dependent more on the quantity and dietary need. Regardless, these emergency stores should be made unavailable until such time as needed.

$$$$$

HEALTH

Again, it is identical to Agriculture. However, rather than having to be USA owned and operated, foreign ownership should be permitted, especially in the case of pharmaceuticals and drugs.

$$$$$

ENERGY

The USA is one of the few Countries in the World that does not have an energy policy or at least one that is all encompassing and coordinated.

In the 1950's and 60's, our Government got the bright idea that rather than industry setting the price of oil, it should be set by our commodity exchanges. The next thing we knew was that if there was more than a three or four-year supply in the market place, commodity traders interpreted that as being a surplus with prices collapsing and wells being shut down with new exploration and drilling abandoned. This despite there being a ten-year lag to bring on new production. However, joy to the traders, for this meant wide swings in prices and masses of speculative profit. There was one minor problem in all of this; the big producers in the Middle East said no thank you to traders in Chicago dictating what kind of profit they would make and the next thing we knew was the OPEC Cartel had been formed! Talk about unintended consequences, this was one for the ages. With prices low at the start, soon domestic industry had almost abandoned exploration followed by a boyish sense of enthusiasm to clean up our environment, ensuring that what little was left be stopped. The scene was now set for future USA shortages to emerge and the inevitable surge in imports and prices dictated by OPEC. As for down-stream industries such as Chemicals, and Fertilizers, the flight to overseas was on.

From 2004 to 2014, a combination of domestic shortages and high prices cost the USA some $2.0 trillion in increased import prices and deficits in our Trading Balances (negative cash flows), not to mention the traumatic job losses and delays in bringing on new production. You can be sure the politicians never admitted this was their fault. Just think all this mess was just in one industry! The incredible fact is that even today, few appreciate what actually happened, and the cost to our country.

Where are we today? Renewable energy is floundering on its own with incentives coming and going on a yearly basis. Pipelines being delayed, while in the meantime shifting transportation to the more dangerous ones of rail and road

$$$$$

HIGH TECH

If we look closely at our domestic USA plants in this category such as Computers, electronics, communications, etc. one finds they are essentially assembly factories that are reliant on imported parts. Virtually all of these imports can be defined as essential investments and having major security implications demanding of a USA manufacturing presence. Reliance on slowing and reversing this position should be a high priority for our Country.

$$$$$

GENERAL

The number one priority should be our Nation's security against both natural, and man-made disasters. Obviously, things like food have to be a priority, but so too do other things, such as military and medical needs. Indeed, if one thinks about it, a whole panoply of goods and services are needed to some degree or other, with a National Security Act perhaps the answer where varying degrees of domestic production would be mandated.

Our Trading Pact Area should not be just the USA, but include all of N. America. Indeed, I personally would support the inclusion of all of Latin with that being the way to stabilize that area as well as it being the ultimate answer to our immigration dilemma. But let's not get ahead of ourselves, for we need to solve our own problems first. (When looking at the Chapter on Geopolitics, please note that virtually all the Countries that make up this area have negative balances of payments with all having the same problem.)

All overseas profits would be allowed a one-time tax write-off exemption if returned to the USA for reinvestment in new plant and equipment.

In addition, in consultation with industry, a re-establishment of key lost industries should be mandated, for this is becoming an increasingly urgent National Security decision.

$$$$$

NOT SERIOUS, BUT NICE

All imports would have to meet the same USA standards for environmental controls, approval procedures for that country's imports and labor working conditions as in the USA.

All farmland would have to meet the requirement of doubling organic soil content within twenty-five years. (Solves 50% of our climate change emissions).

Spying, theft or patent infringement would be considered as grounds to prohibit the further importation of product from that country or company.

Even if only partially implemented, programs of this type would have an immediate and dramatic impact on our balance of Trade, Budgets, and National Debt. Here's hoping our voters are listening and will demand action from their candidates.

$$$$$

IN CASE ANYONE HAS NOT NOTICED, WE HAVE YET TO SUGGEST ANY TARIFF OR DUTY WAR AS NEARLY ALL NATIONS ALREADY DO WHAT WE ARE SUGGESTING AND THE IMPACT ON OUR NATION'S ECONOMY AND BALANCE OF PAYMENTS FROM THE ABOVE WOULD BE INCREDIBLE.

$$$$$

CHAPTER VII

PAYING FOR IT
(GOVERNMENT ACCOUNTING)

On the investment side, one of our ridiculous accounting disconnects should be corrected. In the private sector, investments in buildings and equipment are handled by booking them to assets, and then writing or costing them off over the expected life of those same assets. That way the private sector can afford to make long-term investments which otherwise could never be made from annual income. On the other hand, with Government facing some huge long-term investments, it denies itself the necessity of charging off the entire amount in the year of expenditure. In other words, anything spent on long-term investments is difficult to justify, as it has to be expensed against the current year's budget. In fact, the more expensive something is, the less likely it is ever to be done. To everyone except our politicians a ludicrous situation.

On the other side of this equation, I have been surprised at the practice of our military to give away used equipment when leaving theatres of war. If they were on a depreciation system of costing, where say a tank has a ten-year life, would they leave them behind if they had still five years of costs to write-off? The current system is they have already been written it off, and so there is no cost penalty of abandoning this equipment. On a humorous note, imagine a war in which our Government would have to write-off destroyed equipment. Suddenly we would all know the true cost of that adventure. In case some readers are unfamiliar with what this accounting change would mean, allow me to explain.

Buildings vary from structures built in DC designed to last for sixty years to cheap storage units with a life of twenty years. The two would both be charged off to fixed assets with the cost being depreciated over their expected lives. Likewise, other investments such as dams could be depreciated over their expected lifetimes. Repairs and Maintenance costs would be charged off in two ways, if major and extending the life of the building or another item, it too is added to the cost of that fixed asset, and charged off over its remaining life. Alternatively, if short-term and only to maintain the asset for a year or two, or, if only of minor cost, it would be charged off against the current budget as repairs and maintenance.

In the case of vehicles, planes and other equipment, with expected shorter lives, the results are the same but are spread over say ten to twenty years.

And this is where Moody's calculations went wrong, for these fixed assets more than offset any future liabilities! I don't know what they total other than the fact they must be huge, and so am satisfied to let these omissions offset each other.

$$$$$

I have a request. If any reader of this has connections in high places, or with people that can get this message to the 'doers and shakers,' it would be greatly appreciated if you would pass this onto them, all in the hope it would help solve America's problems.

$$$$$

BIOGRAPHY

My name is Fred Graham-Yooll, and although born and raised in Scotland am a US citizen and make my home in Derwood, Maryland. Educated in Scotland; Edinburgh Academy, Clifton Hall, and Fettes College. In England; Nottingham University, Lt. Royal Artillery. In Canada, joined Northwest Nitro Chemicals, Imperial Oil Ltd, then transferred to the USA with Exxon Mobil Inc. and Esso Malaysia Berhad. In Canada again, as President and CEO of Glacier Ammonia Ltd. Not a believer in retirement, my current enjoyment is golf and writing. 'Cleopatra's Lost Treasure,' Overpopulation, Earth's Destruction and the Fix, The Lost Story of Joseph, and this book.

END NOTES

The special issues heading covers the so-called non-marketable, non-transferable, and non-interest- bearing bonds that are not included in the Federal definition of debt!

Social Security Online

Trust Fund Data

Office of the Chief Actuary

 Investment Holdings
August 17, 2017

Investment holdings

Investment transactions

Trust fund data

The trust funds hold special issues—securities sold only to the trust funds. There are 2 types of such securities: short-term certificates of indebtedness and long-term bonds. The certificates of indebtedness are issued on a daily basis, and they mature on the next June 30 following the date of issue. Special-issue bonds, on the other hand, are normally acquired only when special issues of either type mature on June 30.

In the past, the trust funds have held securities available to the public. Currently, no such public issues are held.

Investments held by the Old-Age, Survivors, and Disability Insurance Trust Funds, at end of year, 2007-2017

Year	Invested amounts (in thousands)				Weighted averages	
		Special Issues				
	Total	Bonds	Certificates of indebtedness	Public Issues	Interest rate (%)	Years to maturity
2007	$2,239,437,635	$2,121,784,895	$117,652,740	$0	5.120	7.279
2008	2,419,213,203	2,331,247,228	87,965,975	0	4.898	7.326
2009	2,518,540,890	2,462,381,505	56,159,385	0	4.688	7.436
2010	2,609,537,218	2,533,221,887	76,315,331	0	4.444	7.407
2011	2,678,894,873	2,610,304,089	68,590,784	0	4.199	7.388
2012	2,733,073,581	2,667,458,740	65,614,841	0	3.856	7.435
2013	2,765,212,571	2,700,548,949	64,663,622	0	3.626	7.466
2014	2,789,581,570	2,728,778,798	60,802,772	0	3.433	7.485
2015	2,786,619,202	2,747,683,764	38,935,438	0	3.225	7.558
2016	2,847,886,510	2,789,066,198	58,820,312	0	3.032	7.497

Note on weighted averages: An average interest rate is weighted by the amount invested at each rate. Similarly, an average number of years to maturity is the time to maturity weighted by the amount for each maturity date.

FEDS Notes

October 8, 2015

Federal Debt in the Financial Accounts of the United States

Marco Cagetti, Matthew Hoops, Susan McIntosh, Rick Ogden

This note explains the concept of federal debt in the *Financial Accounts of the United States*, how it has recently changed, and how it differs from other commonly cited measures of federal debt. As described below, a key factor is the treatment of intragovernmental holdings of U.S. debt securities. In the *Financial Accounts*, the concept of federal government debt includes debt held by the public and intragovernmental holdings in federal government employee defined benefit retirement accounts, but excludes other intragovernmental holdings, such as the Social Security Trust Fund.

The authoritative source for information on U.S. federal debt is Table I of the Treasury Department's *Monthly Statement of the Public Debt* (MSPD), which reports that on June 30, 2015, total public debt outstanding was about $18.2 trillion.[1] Except for some small adjustments, this number also represents the public debt subject to the congressionally mandated debt limit (reported on table II of the MSPD).[2]

Federal debt is categorized as "marketable," such as Treasury bills, notes, bonds, and Treasury inflation-protected securities (TIPS), which can be traded in secondary markets, or "nonmarketable," such as U.S. savings securities, Government Account Series, and State and Local Government Series (SLGS), which cannot be traded. Government Account Series are special securities issued to government trust funds, such as the Social Security Trust Fund, federal employee retirement funds, the Unemployment Trust Fund, etc.

Similarly, federal debt outstanding is categorized as being "intragovernmental," meaning held in government accounts, or "held by the public," meaning all other federal debt. The two concepts of "marketable" debt and debt "held by the public" are closely related--as shown in Table 1 below, the vast majority of marketable debt is held by the public, while the majority of nonmarketable debt is held in intragovernmental accounts. However, some types of nonmarketable debt securities, such as U.S. savings securities, SLGS, and the Thrift Savings Fund are held by the public, and some marketable securities are held intragovernmentally.[3]

In previous publications of the *Financial Accounts*, the concept of federal debt excluded all

Table 1: Treasury securities outstanding on June 30, 2015 (Millions of dollars)

	Debt Held By the Public	Intragovernmental Holdings	Totals
Total Marketable	12,688,996	22,098	12,711,094
Total Nonmarketable	387,418	5,053,486	5,440,904
Total Public Debt Outstanding	13,076,414	5,075,583	18,151,998

Source: Monthly Statement of the Public Debt

Accessible version

intragovernmental holdings and, essentially, included only the debt held by the public. Beginning with the September 18, 2015 publication, the measure of federal debt reported in the *Financial Accounts* has been broadened to include intragovernmental holdings of Treasury securities held by the federal government employee defined benefit retirement funds.[4] This had the effect of adding about $1.3 trillion to the concept of federal debt as of the end of June 2015, raising total federal debt reported in the *Financial Accounts* from $13.2 trillion to about $14.5 trillion.

Note that these intragovernmental holdings of the federal government employee defined benefit retirement funds were previously accounted for in the *Financial Accounts*, but not as federal debt--rather, they were considered miscellaneous assets of the federal government employee defined benefit retirement funds, because intergovernmental nonmarketable Treasury securities were not in the concept of federal debt. The change was made to follow international standards as described in the *System of National Accounts 2008* (SNA2008). Under SNA guidelines, intragovernmental holdings of federal debt are generally excluded from the concept of

OUR WORLD & TRADE

federal debt, but federal government employee defined benefit retirement funds are considered financial corporations and thus not part of the government sector. This same treatment applies to the state and local government employee retirement funds.

Broadly speaking, the concept of federal debt in the *Financial Accounts* now equals Treasury securities held by the public plus intragovernmental holdings in federal government employee defined benefit retirement funds. Importantly, and consistent with SNA guidelines, the *Financial Accounts* concept still does *not* include other intragovernmental holdings, by far the largest of which is the $2.8 trillion Social Security Trust fund. Relative to the topline MSPD numbers in Table 1, we also make a few additional small adjustments to be consistent with *Financial Accounts* concepts. For instance, we net out premiums and discounts (about $55 billion) and include some budget agency securities issued under special financing authorities (about $25 billion).

As shown below in Figure 1, the rate of growth of federal debt is very similar using both the *Financial Accounts* concept and total federal debt reported in the MSPD. The most notable differences are in periods when the debt approaches its statutory limit. During these instances, the Treasury Department can use "extraordinary measures" to temporarily obtain additional room to borrow.[5] Some of these measures involve the suspension of investments into various trust funds. Once the debt limit is increased, the Treasury is required to restore these investments.

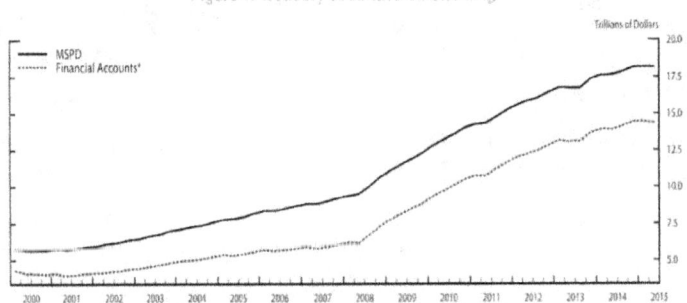

Figure 1: Treasury securities outstanding

Source: Monthly Statement of the Public Debt and Financial accounts of the United States, September 18, 2015

Note: Financial Accounts data includes marketable and nonmarketable Treasury securities held by the public (net of premiums and discounts) and Treasury securities held by federal government employee retirement funds.

Accessible version

The *Financial Accounts* also break down holdings of federal debt by sector.[6] This breakdown comes from a number of data sources, including regulatory reports of many types of financial institutions.[7] As shown in Table 2, the rest of the world sector is the largest holder of U.S. federal debt in the *Financial Accounts*, with over $6 trillion, or 43 percent of federal debt.[8] The monetary authority sector (i.e., the Federal Reserve) is currently the second largest holder, with nearly $2.5 trillion, or 17 percent of the *Financial Accounts* concept of federal debt.[9] The federal government employee retirement funds hold nearly ten percent, most of which is held in intragovernmental accounts.

Table 2: Sectoral distribution of Treasury securities (2015:Q2)

Sector	Value (millions)	Share (percent)
Rest of the world	6,174,273	43.0
Monetary authority	2,460,957	17.1
Federal gov't employee retirement funds	1,381,588	9.6
Households and nonprofit organizations	1,012,985	7.1
Mutual funds	652,033	4.5
State and local governments	641,578	4.5
S&L and private pensions retirement funds	499,834	3.5
U.S.-chartered depository institutions	424,192	3.0
Money market mutual funds	398,094	2.8
Insurance companies	292,591	2.0
Other	415,276	2.9

Source: Monthly Statement of the Public Debt and Financial accounts of the United States, September 18, 2015

Note: Financial Accounts data includes marketable and nonmarketable Treasury securities held by the public (net of premiums and discounts) and Treasury securities held by federal government employee retirement funds.

Accessible version